PERGAMON

THYATIRA

SMYRNA

SARDIS

PHILADELPHIA

EPHESUS

LAODICEA

GERMANY
CZECH REP.
SLOVAKIA
UKRAINE
FRANCE
SWITZERLAND
AUSTRIA
HUNGARY
SLOVENIA
CROATIA
ROMANIA
BOSNIA
AND
HERZ.
SERBIA
MONTENEGRO
BULGARIA
ITALY
MACEDONIA
ALBANIA
ARMENIA
GREECE
TURKEY
MALTA
SYRIA
CYPRUS
LEBANON
IRAQ
ALGERIA
TUNISIA
ISRAEL
JORDAN
LIBYA
EGYPT

"René Schlaepfer is a master storyteller. The treat of this book is that René takes us on an archeological exploration of Jesus' letters to the church, and along the way the Gospel's story for contemporary Christians comes alive."

Rev. Dr. M. Craig Barnes, president of Princeton Theological Seminary and author of *When God Interrupts, Sacred Thirst, Searching For Home,* and *The Pastor as Minor Poet*

"Once again, René brings us on an adventure into the fascinating history of the ancient world — but brings to life the contemporary application for today. Your life will experience both deep encouragement as well as some healthy conviction and you will never read the first chapters of Revelation the same way again."

Dan Kimball, author of *Adventures in Churchland* and *They Like Jesus But Not The Church*

"René Schlaepfer's latest book, *The Seven,* has opened the Book of Revelation to me in a way none other has. The author's easy-to-read style and insightful teaching will stir your mind and heart to take in the words of Jesus that are as fresh and applicable to Christians today as they were to followers in the early church. Don't miss this book."

Karen O'Connor, author of *When God Answers Your Prayers; Lord, How Did I Get This Old So Soon?;* and many more

"René takes you back through time and space as he visits actual sites mentioned in the Book of Revelation. What do the mysterious words of Revelation 2 and 3 mean? They've puzzled me for years! René's angle, looking at the latest archaeological research for clues — not clues about the future, but about the past — brings new light to these riddles. I recommend it!"

Bill Butterworth, speaker and author of *The Short List, Balancing Life and Work*, and more

"As someone who tends to camp in the "easier" parts of the New Testament, I'm blown away by René Schlaepfer's *The Seven*. For the first time, I am actually excited about delving into Revelation and understanding what Jesus meant in the light of the political and cultural issues of the time. I feel like a secret part of the Scriptures has been unlocked for me. Highly recommended."

Kathi Lipp, author of *The Cure for the Perfect Life* and *Clutter Free*

"THE SEVEN: HOPE FROM JESUS IN THE BOOK OF REVELATION"

© 2015 René Schlaepfer

ISBN 978-1-4951-7051-5

1st printing: 2015

Unless otherwise indicated, Scripture quotations are from:

THE HOLY BIBLE, NEW INTERNATIONAL VERSION®, NIV®

Copyright © 1973, 1978, 1984, 2011 by Biblica, Inc.™

Used by permission. All rights reserved worldwide.

Scripture quotations marked NLT are taken from the Holy Bible, New Living Translation, copyright © 1996, 2004, 2007 by Tyndale House Foundation. Used by permission of Tyndale House Publishers, Inc., Carol Stream, Illinois 60188. All rights reserved.

Scripture quotations marked "MSG" or "The Message" are taken from The Message. Copyright 1993, 1994, 1995, 1996, 2000, 2001, 2002. Used by permission of NavPress Publishing Group.

Unless otherwise indicated, all photos are credited to David Schlaepfer, Jamie Rom, or part of the public domain.

Printed locally on recycled paper with soy-based inks at Community Printers, Santa Cruz, CA.

If you would like to reproduce or distribute any part of this publication, please contact:

Twin Lakes Church, 2701 Cabrillo College Drive, Aptos, CA 95003-3103, USA

or email info@tlc.org

THE SEVEN

HOPE FROM JESUS IN THE BOOK OF REVELATION

CONTENTS

NOTE TO READERS

This book is designed to be read in 50 short daily sections, but of course you can power through it all at once if you prefer. It also ties into a message series and videos at www.tlc.org/theseven

When I travelled to the actual sites of these seven churches I recorded video discussion starters at each location. So if you'd like to see what these places look like today and get some additional study material for your small group or personal study, you can download and watch the videos for free, also at www.tlc.org/theseven

INTRODUCTION

THE SEVEN

The Book of Revelation. The last book of the Bible. And the most mysterious.

Filled with cryptic references to the final battles between good and evil, Revelation has inspired countless guesses about the identity of the Antichrist, the date of Armageddon, and the time of Christ's return. Seen primarily as a book of prophecy about future events, it has captured our imagination for centuries.

Michelangelo painted scenes from Revelation on the walls of the Sistine Chapel.

Dante's *Divine Comedy* was inspired by Revelation.

Songs by Nirvana ("Lake of Fire"), Iron Maiden ("The Number of the Beast") and Prince ("7byPrince") quote the book directly.

The best-selling *Left Behind* book series dramatizes parts of Revelation.

The 1970 book *The Late Great Planet Earth* compared current events to Revelation's prophecies to prove we were living in the end times.

The author even speculated the rapture might happen in the 1980s (He was wrong, but his guess was really good for book sales).

And that's just a brief sample.

MISSING THE POINT
Frankly I have a problem with many of these approaches to the book. And it's this: Most miss the big picture. The kaleidoscope of spooky imagery in all these songs, stories, and sculptures can make Revelation seem like a scary nightmare.

But the Book of Revelation has just one overarching theme: To let persecuted Christians know, God's got your back. He is still in control, even if everything seems chaotic now.

Then sometimes I get impatient with the way people approach Revelation for another reason. Nearly all the songs, paintings, sculptures, books, and movies focus on the weirdest parts of the book: The beasts and battles. Very few people seem to notice the first three chapters. In fact, I don't know of a single story or song or sculpture based on this section.

Maybe that's because we'd rather just overlook these chapters. They hit too close to home. Because they are written not about God's reaction to giant evil systems and serpents and Satan, but about God's reaction to... you and me.

STRESS AND STRAIN
When Revelation was written, back around the end of the first century, there were scattered persecutions of Christians throughout the Roman Empire. Depending on how determined the local authorities were to act on Caesar's commands, Christians could face imprisonment and even death — or fly completely under the radar.

Naturally, this kind of uncertainty led to a lot of stress. Christians in cities where persecution was hot might have felt abandoned by God. Christians in places where the living was easier might have felt uniquely approved by God.

The early chapters of Revelation address all these people. People like you and me. Some confused by life, feeling hammered, suspecting Jesus is never going to come back. Others smug and self-satisfied, sinking into self-centered religion. And still others who want to follow God but find the busyness of life fleecing them of the freedom they once felt in their faith.

They are all addressed in seven letters to seven different churches, dictated to John by Jesus in a vision, and recorded in Revelation chapters 2 and 3.

There's been a lot written about the latter part of Revelation. And maybe I'll write something about that one day too. But in this book I want to focus on this first part, the overlooked part, the part specifically addressed to you and me today, to whoever has "ears to hear" what Jesus says in seven letters to seven churches. I call this little-known section of the Bible *The Seven*.

CRACKING THE CODE

Here's the biggest obstacle to understanding the Book of Revelation: John writes in all kinds of cryptic symbols and codes. Revelation is written in a genre called apocalyptic literature. It was very popular in the first century A.D. and consisted of messages conveyed through dream-like poetic imagery.

Clearly, the original people reading Revelation understood it. It encouraged and enlightened them. Otherwise, they would have just thrown it away instead of passing it all around the Empire and preserving it as inspired Scripture.

But because it's such a product of its time, Revelation looks really strange to modern readers. The codes are tough to crack unless you know what the original readers knew about the Hebrew Bible and Roman history.

It's like this: Imagine an archaeologist 2,000 years from now finding a newspaper from the 21st century and reading a political cartoon. He sees an elephant and a donkey with gloves on, fighting in a boxing ring with a circular logo — an eagle surrounded by stars — on the floor. The donkey has short blonde hair. The elephant is strangely faceless.

He might conclude that people used to love watching fights between genetically modified animals. In fact, unless he knows the political scene in 2015, he would never guess that the cartoon is a reference to the Democrats (the donkey) and the Republicans (the elephant) duking it out in yet another presidential election (the presidential seal on the floor). The donkey has a short blonde haircut signifying the presumed Democratic nominee Hilary Clinton, while the elephant is faceless because the Republican nominee, at the time the cartoon was drawn, had yet to be decided.

The Book of Revelation is a little like a political cartoon from the first century. Unless you know what certain symbols stood for in that society (the equivalent of our elephant, donkey, and eagle) and what was going on historically right in that moment, you will never understand its subtleties. But to people living then, the meaning was clear.

THE DECODING TOUR

That's why, to prepare for this book, I took a trip to the original sites of the seven churches with a study group from our church. Just seeing the geography, ruins, and surviving art in those locations cleared up many points of confusion for me, as you'll see.

And we travelled with Tulu Gökkadar, a teacher from that very region of Turkey who lectures on the Historical Geography of Asia Minor and is currently completing her Master's degree in Classical Archaeology. You can imagine the immense help she was in decoding the historical references in Revelation.

Much of what I discovered on my trip truly surprised me. I want to share these discoveries with you in these pages. Because the message of Christ in these mysterious letters needs desperately to be heard by Christians today.

But apocalyptic literature is not just about Roman history. It also contains lots of references to the Hebrew Bible or Old Testament, especially the books of Isaiah and Daniel. If you are familiar with those books and with first-century history, much of what seems like cryptic code can be cracked.

Happily, the overall message of Revelation — despite suffering, victory is promised in Jesus Christ! — is clear even if you don't decode the details. But if you do understand those references, these verses really pop to life.

MESSAGES FROM JESUS

Think about it. What if you got a text message right now — from Jesus?

And what if, in his text, he wrote very brief, to-the-point words about exactly what you need to keep thriving spiritually?

What kinds of things do you think he might say to you?

Where would he correct you? What would he say to encourage you?

And what do you suppose he might think of the churches around the world that claim to follow him?

In the first three chapters of the Book of Revelation, that's exactly what happens: We get brief messages from Christ designed to help you thrive spiritually, starting today! Some of his words in these letters are encouraging. Others are challenging. But they are all words of hope. Because even in the call to repent, or the warning of trials, Jesus offers hope - the certainity that God is in control, and promises a future for those who love him that is brighter than any of us can imagine.

☰ APPLY IT

At the very start and the very end of these seven letters, Jesus says this:

> *"Anyone with ears to hear must listen to the Spirit and understand what he is saying to the churches."* REV. 3:22

Ask God to help you listen to the Spirit so you can understand what he is saying to you though this study of the seven churches.

1

FINDING PEACE
IN THE CHAOS

Freaked out and afraid.

Frankly that's how a lot of folks I know are reacting to life right now. Easy to see why.

Shooting, unrest, and fear in America.

Europe in financial turmoil.

The Middle East in chaos.

Wars, rumors of wars, and remnants of wars in Iraq, Afghanistan, Syria, and Libya.

And this frightening fact: Persecution of Christians worldwide has spiraled to unparalleled levels.

So yeah, freaking out is an understandable response.

Especially since it all feels so intense and immediate. Thanks to 24-hour news channels and the vast connectivity of the internet, our phones, laptops, and even watches buzz with blasts of bad news as it happens. Sometimes it feels like we have a God's-eye view of every sin, scandal, and stumble all around the world. And our human nervous systems just can't handle omniscience. So what do we do?

The usual responses are anxiety or apathy. You either stay connected and get weirded out and worried, or you disconnect and live the life of a head-hiding ostrich.

But there's another option.

See, we actually don't have a God-eye view of the problems. True, God sees all the bad stuff happening. But he also sees the vastly bigger picture: He will set all things right. And he is with us right now, showing us how to live in the meantime.

The Book of Revelation paints that picture, using poetic, dream-like imagery. But it's a picture just as real as the vivid images you see on your TV or phone screen.

Revelation was written to people going through intense times of change and unrest too. The first-century Roman world was a very insecure place for the fledgling Christian movement. A lot of Christians were choosing those two options of anxiety or apathy. So God sends a set of visions to the one remaining original apostle, John, to give them the bigger picture. The real picture. And in the text of the first three chapters are clues for you and me about how to survive and thrive in a sometimes scary world.

Here's how it unfolds.

THE ISLAND

It's near the end of the first century. Eleven of the twelve original disciples of Jesus are dead, killed for their faith. Only John remains. And he's been exiled to a small rocky island in the Aegean Sea called Patmos, simply for the crime of being Christian.

These days the blue-green Aegean is a popular vacation destination, but back then exile to an island like this was a severe punishment.

The historian William Ramsay details how grueling these prison islands could be:

> Such banishment would be preceded by scourging, marked
> by perpetual fetters, scanty clothing, insufficient food,
> sleeping on bare ground in a dark prison cave, working
> under the lash of a military overseer... [1]

HOPE WHEN TIMES ARE TOUGH

Imagine it. John is alone. He's impoverished. He's weak. All the other apostles, his closest friends, are dead. He is very elderly, probably in his nineties. He must have been so lonely. And so worried about the churches back on the mainland.

But then he thinks about his best friend. Jesus. And the one thing that brings him hope: He will see Jesus again! The Lord will make all things right, despite the mess the world's in now!

And he writes a letter about this, addressed to churches back on the mainland. It's this letter that we call the Book of Revelation. It was meant to inspire these Christians living under threat of persecution. Many of them must have felt like God had passed them by. Like they were living a doomed life. They were feeling rejected and unvalued. So John starts by describing our hope in Christ:

> *All glory to him who loves us and has freed us from our sins by*
> *shedding his blood for us.* REV. 1:5B NLT

John begins with the gospel. This is the foundation of all our hope. Jesus loves you. He gave everything to set you free. And he promises to finish what he started.

---

1   William Barclay, *The Revelation of John, Volume 1*, St. Andrews Press, 1965, p. 52

*He has made us a Kingdom of priests for God his Father. All glory
and power to him forever and ever! Amen.*

*Look! He comes with the clouds of heaven.
     And everyone will see him —
     even those who pierced him.*

*And all the nations of the world
     will mourn for him.*

Yes! Amen!

*"I am the Alpha and the Omega—the beginning and the end," says
the Lord God. "I am the one who is, who always was, and who is
still to come — the Almighty One."* REV. 1:6-8 NLT

HE'S COMING BACK

John is so excited and encouraged by this truth: Jesus is going to
return.

Did you know that the return of Jesus is one of the most frequently
mentioned truths in the whole New Testament? In its 260 chapters,
there are 318 references to Christ's return. One out of every 30 verses
in the New Testament contains some sort of reference or allusion to
the return of Jesus. For every prophecy about the first advent of the
Messiah, there are 8 about the second advent!

Yet most Christians don't think about it much today. Too bad, because
this can bring so much hope when life seems to be going badly off the
rails.

Ray Johnston tells the story of Allied prisoners in a POW camp during
World War II. They received word through underground contacts that
the war was essentially over; the Germans were about to surrender. For
three days before their camp was liberated, they smiled at the attack
dogs, waved at their captors, and were generally in a jubilant mood.

Their situation hadn't changed at all. But they knew what was coming! And three days later they woke up to find the guards gone, the gates open, and they simply walked out to freedom.

The point: When you know how things will turn out, it changes you.

Do you believe that Jesus not just "was" or even "is", but is "still to come"? Do you believe he will return to set all things right? What you believe really makes a difference. Imagine the impact this would make on your struggles with suffering, self-doubt, sadness, sickness, and sin. Believe it: All this will end in victory when the Alpha and Omega, Jesus Christ, returns to make all things new!

≡ APPLY IT

How does the idea of the return of Christ make you feel? Confident? Nervous? Inspired? Confused?

How do you hope to change during this study of the Book of Revelation?

2

A VISIT FROM A FRIEND

Why is John so excited about the return of Christ? Because he's had a visitor.

As he is worshipping, John hears a voice behind him commanding,

> *"Write in a book everything you see, and send it to the seven churches in the cities of Ephesus, Smyrna, Pergamum, Thyatira, Sardis, Philadelphia, and Laodicea."* REV. 1:11

These seven churches were all in Asia Minor — not the continent we call Asia, but the Roman province of Asia where modern Turkey exists today. They were all on the same circular trade route, like a loop road. If you started at Ephesus and went clockwise, you'd reach each of these cities in the exact order they're listed in this verse.

Remember, when John hears this voice he's alone on the island. And as he spins around to see who said these words, he has the surprise of his life:

> *"When I turned to see who was speaking to me, I saw seven gold lampstands. And standing in the middle of the lampstands was someone like the Son of Man. He was wearing a long robe with a gold sash across his chest. His head and his hair were white like*

wool, as white as snow. And his eyes were like flames of fire. His feet were like polished bronze refined in a furnace, and his voice thundered like mighty ocean waves. He held seven stars in his right hand, and a sharp two-edged sword came from his mouth. And his face was like the sun in all its brilliance.

"When I saw him, I fell at his feet as if I were dead. But he laid his right hand on me and said, "Don't be afraid! I am the First and the Last. I am the living one. I died, but look — I am alive forever and ever! And I hold the keys of death and the grave." REV. 1:12-18 NLT

This first vision of Jesus Christ is actually not a future vision; it's a *present* vision. These verses don't say, "This is what Jesus Christ will one day be like and what He will do in the future." They are all about what He is like *now* and what He is doing *now*.

This is huge. John doesn't start with hellfire and scolding. He starts with a breathtaking, mind-boggling vision of the living Christ.

Only when my imagination is captured by the powerful beauty of Jesus and how he set me free am I motivated to go the direction he points me. The Bible *always* starts here first. Parts of this first description are repeated in each of the seven letters — and I'll comment on all the symbolism then — but right now I'll elaborate on just a couple details.

TOUGH TIMES

First, some context: Most scholars believe Revelation was written around 90-96 AD, during the final years of the reign of Domitian.[2] These were tough years for early believers.

According to the ancient Roman writer Suetonius, Domitian's rule started well, but gradually declined into terror and paranoia. He was

---

2 A minority of scholars believe Revelation was composed earlier, around 69 AD, during the first intense persecution of the church by Nero. The Roman historian Tacitus records how Nero slaughtered "a great multitude of Christians" then. Peter and Paul were killed during this period. Whether during Nero's reign or Domitian's, Revelation was written in the context of intense state pressure on the young Christian movement.

the first Roman Emperor who demanded he be addressed as *Dominus et Deus*, Latin for "Lord and God" (Those self-esteem lessons must have really worked!). If you didn't worship him (and most Christians refused) you were killed, imprisoned, or ostracized.

So where was God while all this was happening?

RIGHT HERE WITH US

In verse 20, Jesus himself explains part of the vision: He says the seven golden lampstands represent the seven churches.

But look at the details. The lampstands are *golden.* What's that signify? In Roman times, as now, gold was the most precious, most beautiful, most valuable metal. This means that though Caesar may reject them, believers are, to the heart of Jesus, the most precious, the most beautiful, most valuable thing on the earth.

And what is he doing there among the lampstands? This is so awesome! *He is standing in the middle of them.* He is not looking down on them from afar. *He is with us.* He promised he would always be with us, and he is! This imagery is meant to encourage you that Jesus is right there beside you as you read, right here with me as I write.

When you experience your own difficult days and dark nights, remember that God is not on vacation. He is not far away, oblivious to your struggles. He is right here. He will never leave you nor forsake you.

ANCIENT OF DAYS

And notice: *"His head and His hair were white like wool, like snow".*

This is a reference to the Book of Daniel. Writing several centuries before Christ, Daniel records a vision of God, the "Ancient of Days", sitting down to judge the nations, and describes him like this: *"His clothing was as white as snow, his hair like purest wool."* (DANIEL 7:19) Of course this is not meant to suggest that if you saw God, he would actually have white hair, any more than that political cartoon I mentioned earlier is meant to prove Republicans all look like elephants.

Because the more literal parts of the Bible teach that God is spirit and does not actually have a physical body, we know this is symbolic language. White hair in those days symbolized wisdom (Hey! I must be very wise!) and white clothing stood for holiness. So this means that God is the wisest and holiest being in the universe. And this is crucial: By applying Daniel's description of God to Jesus Christ, John is saying *Jesus is in fact God.*

In other words, no matter what it may seem like right now, Domitian is not "Lord and God". Jesus is! Domitian does not have the final word of judgment. Jesus does! He's the one in charge, not Domitian or any other human.

THE SWORD OF AUTHORITY

John says a sword came out of Jesus' mouth. Again, this is a symbol, like that political cartoon. The sword imagery stood for something. And everyone knew what.

The will of Caesar was put into effect by the powerful Roman governors that ruled each province. And the governor's power was called "the right of the sword" – the Latin expression is *ius gladii*. This meant that the governor, and only the governor, had the power of life or death over the people.

This vision is making the case that the ultimate power of life and death is not in the Roman government's hands. It's in the hand of Jesus Christ.

All the other aspects of this vision represent the authority and power of Jesus too. The feet of bronze, the seven stars, and all the other symbols can be interpreted if you know what those symbols meant to the people of that time. I promise we'll cover them in more detail later in this book, but the big idea is this: Jesus is ultimately in charge of history, and is right here with us, right now!

YOUR FOCUS CHANGES YOUR EXPECTATION

Why would John start a letter to persecuted Christians with this description of Jesus? Same reason each of the seven letters that come next starts this way: What you focus on changes what you expect. Focus on God's power and you expect victory. A simple shift in what you choose to focus on can move you from despair to hope.

≡ APPLY IT

Do you ever despair when you look at the world's headlines — or situations in your own life?

How can this vision of Jesus encourage you?

Some of the spectacular ruins of Ephesus

DIGGING DEEPER

Don't get the impression that all books of the Bible are written in some secret code. Most are very straight-forward. You don't need some special knowledge to understand Romans or Galatians, for example.

But the few apocalyptic books (Revelation in the New Testament and parts of Daniel and Isaiah in the Old Testament) are deliberately written in almost dream-like imagery that had symbolic associations for the people to whom these books were written. The more we know about their culture, the better we can understand the symbols.

Apocalyptic literature is a genre that emerged a few centuries before Christ. First-century Jews would have been very familiar with this literary form. Even non-Jewish Christians would have recognized the genre, because it was used among other cultures as well.

Writers of apocalyptic works usually wrote in the name of heroes from Israel's history. There are many books written in this style that are not in the Bible. Some are ascribed to Enoch, Abraham, the Twelve Patriarchs, Moses, Ezra, and Elijah, among others.

Dream-like, symbolic imagery is one characteristic of apocalyptic literature. It's also typified by common themes. Apocalyptic works claim to reveal God's purpose in history. In particular, these works try to explain why the righteous suffer and why God seems to be delaying his final justice. These writings were what commentators call "tracts for hard times."

Revelation differs a little from most non-Biblical apocalyptic works, which tend to be very dualistic: Two equal but opposite supernatural powers are doing battle. Revelation has lots of battle scenes, but in this book, God has no equal. The evil powers arrayed against the righteous are seen as puny and doomed to fail.

THE FIRST LETTER

3

TO BUSY CHRISTIANS

I can't believe what's unfolding in front of me. I've come to the ancient ruins of Ephesus, one of the most beautiful archaeological sites in the world and the first of the seven cities Jesus addresses in the Book of Revelation.

The city sparkles even after centuries under grit and grime that's slowly being scraped away by a team of archaeologists. Spectacular marble reliefs and intricate tile mosaics are emerging from the mud and dust, like ancient flowers blooming once more.

One of the most massive structures in Ephesus today is the crumbling temple originally built to worship the Emperor Domitian. Only the terrace on which the temple stood remains. But this supporting structure alone is huge, the length and width of a football field, built on vaulted foundations that are still two stories high. As I walk past, I try to imagine the awe-inspiring temple that once loomed far above this plaza. It must have seemed impossible to resist the power of the emperor who built this imposing edifice to deify himself.

But what fascinates me about the ruins of Ephesus is not just the massive ruins. I'm equally intrigued by the intricate details being slowly uncovered by the archaeologist's spades.

Like the bees.

On statues, coins, buildings, and home decorations, bee imagery was common in ancient Ephesus. They loved bees here. The bee was what we would call today the brand or logo of Ephesus, associated with the city in many ways.

Our guide Tulu tells me that the bee was associated with Ephesus for many reasons.

Ancient Ephesian coin with symbol of the city, the bee

The priestesses of Artemis were called bees. Legend held that bees led the first colonists to the city. And the Ephesians admired the work ethic of bees.

Ephesus was a glamorous, busy city. It was across the Aegean Sea from Athens, in a picturesque location, with a vibrant port. It's still very impressive.

When I walked through its ruins I was in awe of the culture that produced its beautifully paved streets, the massive theater with seating for 25,000 spectators, the stunning library façade, and the recently excavated homes of the Ephesian elite. The two-story houses had huge central courtyards, hot and cold running water, huge living and dining rooms, and clay pipes under the floors and behind the walls which carried hot air from furnaces to heat the homes in cold weather. The intricacy of detail in the surviving statues and mosaics is breathtaking.

One look around these ruins and you realize: This was a city of over-achievers. They were on top of the heap. They lived in what was considered one of the most beautiful cities in the world.

And apparently the Christians at Ephesus took on this aspect of their culture. They were over-achievers, straight-A students.

It's an unintended consequence of that tendency toward busyness that Jesus addresses in his first letter to the seven churches.

BUSY AS BEES

We too live in a super-busy culture. Would you say your life right now is busier than ever?

Consider these stats: People now sleep two-and-a-half fewer hours each night than people did a century ago. The average work week is far longer now than in the 1960s. According to a report by ABC News, not only are Americans working longer hours than at any time since statistics have been kept, but they are also working longer than anyone else in the industrialized world.

And think of how busy you are outside work, with sports, hobbies, chores, helping kids with homework — and even at church.

Yet a busy lifestyle is not always productive spiritually. In fact, it can drain your love for God and for others.

If that sounds familiar, Jesus has words for me and for you:

"To the angel of the church in Ephesus write:"

And here let me just mention that the Greek word translated *"angel"* can refer either to a heavenly messenger or a human one. It simply means "the bearer of news". I believe it refers to human messengers here. Why would Jesus dictate a message first to John in order to pass it on to heavenly beings? Jesus is asking John to record these letters onto parchment in order to give physical letters to human messengers who will take the letters from the island to the mainland.

> *"These are the words of him who holds the seven stars in his right hand and walks among the seven golden lampstands. I know your deeds, your hard work and your perseverance. I know that you cannot tolerate wicked people, that you have tested those who claim to be apostles but are not, and have found them false. You have persevered and have endured hardships for my name, and have not grown weary.*
>
> *"Yet I hold this against you: You have forsaken the love you had at first. Consider how far you have fallen! Repent and do the things you did at first. If you do not repent, I will come to you and remove your lampstand from its place.*
>
> *"But you have this in your favor: You hate the practices of the Nicolaitans, which I also hate.*
>
> *"Whoever has ears, let them hear what the Spirit says to the churches. To the one who is victorious, I will give the right to eat from the tree of life, which is in the paradise of God."* REV. 2:1-7 NIV

Each of the seven letters follows the same format (with only a couple exceptions): They all start with a majestic description of Jesus, then move on to a commendation of good things that church is doing, a condemnation of bad stuff the church is involved with, and end with a promise of victory for those who apply the message.

I love the fact that in the very first letter of The Seven, before he deals with churches who were compromising morally or theologically, Jesus talks about the simplest yet most important thing of all: Our love for God. If that's not right, then nothing else is right. That's the foundation for all the correction that comes later.

C. S. Lewis said, "Every Christian would agree that a man's spiritual health is exactly proportional to his love for God." [3]

So how's your spiritual love life?

LOSING YOUR FIRST LOVE

The Ephesians seemed to have it all together. Persecution was endured with dignity. False doctrine was handled with truth. Immorality was resisted with holiness. The thing that tripped up the straight-A Ephesians was far subtler. Their love had grown cold.

Maybe you can relate. I know I can.

I usually seem to handle life's major problems, even deaths and disease, with resolve (so far!). I am determined to stay doctrinally focused on the essentials of the Christian faith. What stalls out my Christian life is not usually suffering or persecution or false teaching.

It's a subtle shift in focus — a shift from my *love* for God to the things I *do* for God. From the great *I Am* to the great *To Do*. From the Lord to the List. From his daily grace to my daily grind.

I don't abandon the faith or curse God. I just get so busy *for* Him I can forget to be *with* Him. I still do the right things and believe the right things, but my heart grows cold.

How to get the love back? That's next.

≡ APPLY IT

We'll look at this letter throughout the week, but for now ask yourself this: Have I lost the vibrancy of my first love for Jesus? Has my focus shifted from the great *I Am* to the great *To Do*? Pray that God will help you rediscover your first love this week.

---

3   C.S. Lewis, *The Four Loves*. Inspirational Press: New York, 1984. p. 214

4

HE SEES AND HE CARES

Ever wonder if God sees your good deeds?

Maybe you're taking care of an elderly loved one at home and you wonder if anyone knows or cares about the thousandth time you have bitten your tongue and taken care of an "accident."

Maybe you're a working parent and you wonder if anyone knows or cares about all the endless time put into cooking, cleaning, and helping with homework.

Or you may be suffering yourself, the victim of a disease, doing your best to keep your spirits high. Does anyone know how hard it is?

Jesus begins his letter to the Ephesians with some very encouraging words. He sees. He knows. And He cares.

> *"These are the words of him who holds the seven stars in his right hand and walks among the seven golden lampstands."* REV. 2:1 NLT

Let's decode this. John starts with an easy one. In this case we know the seven stars are the angels, or representatives, of the seven local churches because Jesus has just identified them as such to John in the immediately preceding verse, Revelation 1:20 (there's another intriguing meaning every Roman would have seen in a reference to seven stars, which we'll talk about when it comes up later).

In the previous verse Jesus already identified the seven lampstands as the churches themselves. The point is that all these Christians, in all these various situations — some rich, some poor, some in trouble, some in comfort — were all in his hands: he *"holds"* us. We're all in his presence: he *"walks among"* us.

The takeaway? Don't carry what is not yours to carry. It's all in Jesus' hands. You are in *His* hands. Your future is in *His* hands. Your church is in *His* hands. Maybe you're worried because you're trying to carry something around right now that isn't yours to carry.

> *"I know all the things you do. I have seen your hard work and your patient endurance. I know you don't tolerate evil people. You have examined the claims of those who say they are apostles but are not. You have discovered they are liars. You have patiently suffered for me without quitting."* REV. 2:2-3 NLT

So Jesus knows they are:

• SERVING

The Ephesians were famous for their deeds. Spiritual bumblebees. Always working. And Jesus says, "I appreciate that." The Greek translated "hard work" means, "to labor to the point of exhaustion." Not only did they work. They worked overtime. They didn't just do what the job required. They went above and beyond the call of duty.

• STEADFAST

Jesus commends them for "patient endurance." They were consistent. They didn't quit. He says, in essence, "I know you've been doing your job in the church nursery or the food pantry or your own home, day after day, week after week, year after year. You've hung in there. Great job!"

• SCHOLARLY

They were religiously educated. They knew their doctrine. They were discerning about the teaching they followed. Orthodox to the core.

• SUFFERING

They hung in there, even through tough times, patiently, without quitting.

It's sometimes easy in a study of these seven letters to focus only on the verses that have a *condemnation*. But we also need to look at the *commendation*.

Jesus sees your life. He knows your suffering. He appreciates your good deeds. In fact, he told his disciples that even a cup of cold water given in his name would receive a reward in his kingdom. That means the smallest act of kindness, something you will probably never remember yourself, is remembered by the Lord.

The old Scottish writer Robert Murray M'Cheyne, in his book on Revelation, put it this way:

> Every believer feels that his own works are nothing, and it is right that he should feel so, because he feels there is so much vileness in everything he does — such a mixture of motives. For example, if you were to be kind to a stranger, you may have in doing so but one grain of love for Christ, and a hundred grains of other motivations; perhaps love of praise, or a desire to be well thought of. Now I will tell you what Christ does; He sprinkles the hundred grains with his own blood, he forgets them all, and treasures up the one grain of love to himself, and says unto you, "I know thy works, and thy labour, and thy patience." [4]

---

4   Robert Murray M'Cheyne, *The Seven Churches of Asia*, p. 9

≡ APPLY IT

Thank God today that you are in his hands. And he sees and he knows every act of kindness and service you do, even with mixed motives. How does that motivate and encourage you?

DIGGING DEEPER

n Revelation 2:6, Jesus also mentions a group called the Nicolaitans. Although our understanding of them is very limited because so few descriptions of them survive, this was apparently a group that claimed to follow the teaching of a man named Nicholas.

According to the early church fathers, Nicholas taught a form of dualism which said the physical body is corrupt, but the spirit is pure. So, he concluded, whatever people do physically does not impact who they are spiritually. He apparently even encouraged his disciples to be immoral in order to showcase how little they cared about the physical world, and to demonstrate the power of God's grace to save their spirits.

But this is not what the Bible teaches. The physical and spiritual parts of our lives are both important to God, created by God, and can be redeemed by God. This is one reason it's important to understand that the Bible teaches a complete resurrection, physical and not just spiritual. God promises a restoration of heaven and earth as our eternal dwelling place, not just a home for our spirits.

There have been times that Christians have despised the physical side of life, wrongly thinking that the internal spiritual life is the only thing that matters to God. But the truth is, God loves all of you, body and spirit.

5

THE POINT OF THE DANCE

I s there a dark side to the stereotypical Silicon Valley super-achieving lifestyle?

In the *Harvard Business Review* article, "Leadership Run Amuck: The Destructive Potential of Overachievers," the authors write:

> Overachieving leaders may be very successful, but there's a dark side... By relentlessly focusing on tasks and goals... an executive may be oblivious to the concerns of others... demolish trust... and undermine morale. We've seen very talented leaders crash and burn as they put ever more pressure on themselves and others to produce. They can be arrogant, aloof, and demanding. [5]

In other words, they remember the goals but forget the relationships.

Jesus has a similar critique for the overachieving Ephesian church. After thanking them for all the wonderful ways they are serving him, Jesus points out one fatal flaw that could lead to worse things down the road if they don't take care of it now:

---

5   Scott Spreier, Mary H. Fontaine, and Ruth Malloy, "Leadership Run Amuck: The Destructive Potential of Overachievers", *Harvard Business Review*, June 2006, accessed at https://hbr.org/2006/06/leadership-run-amok-the-destructive-potential-of-overachievers

"But I have this complaint against you. You don't love me or each other as you did at first!" REV. 2:4 NLT

LOSING MY LOVE

Busy people often need to work on relationships. Including our relationship with God. If we forget that foundation, even the good things we accomplish will begin to sour.

A while ago I got this email from a college senior:

> I have lost a lot of my passion for God. Ever since I went
> back to college and got involved with Christian stuff here on
> campus, I have seen nothing but just a loss in passion.
> I hate it. I can feel a distance between me and the Lord.
> The ministry I am involved with on campus — all the
> meetings, gatherings, the stuff we do... I used to be so excited
> to serve the Lord, with such passion, but I don't know where
> it went. I feel like I am not myself. Help.

Later I'll share with you an email he wrote several months later, but can you relate? I can. I've been there.

Here are some questions to ask yourself. The answers might indicate that you're losing your first love:

- Do you find yourself untouched by worship most of the time?

- Do you find yourself exhausted and resentful when serving?

- Do you often feel unappreciated?

- Are you getting judgmental?

- Do you view Christ's commands as restrictions on your happiness?

- Are you unmoved by the needs of others?

It's important to note that "first love" is not about performance. The Ephesian church was performing with excellence. First love is about intimacy.

CHOOSE THE BETTER PART

It reminds me of the story of Mary and Martha. One sister, Martha, is busily serving in the kitchen. The other sister, Mary, is sitting with Jesus listening to his teaching. And Martha gets really ticked off. She finally cannot stand it any more and says to Jesus, "Tell her to help me!" But Jesus says,

> "Martha, Martha, you are worried and upset about many things, but few things are needed — really only one. Mary has chosen the better part." LUKE 10:41-42

The very "daily-ness" of service can sometimes cause you to lose sight of the reason for the service in the first place: Your love for the One who first loved you, overflowing in love to others.

DANCE LESSONS

I remember when I first learned to dance. I was in sixth grade Physical Education. Remember the humiliation of grade school P.E.? Well, dance lessons made it worse.

I recall the coach's harsh voice through the amplified megaphone: "All right students! Dance! Do the steps I taught, now! One! And two! And three! And repeat!"

Why in the world does anyone like dancing? I thought to myself as I awkwardly held hands with a girl I barely knew. I tried not to make eye contact with her while I mechanically repeated the steps. I just did not understand why people would ever like to dance.

A few years later when I fell in love... and held my girlfriend close... I understood! I actually did some of the very same dance steps, but, wow, what a difference.

LOVE THE DANCER

You may have been taught the essentials of the Christian life by people who were a lot like the Ephesians. High achievers who just wanted the best for you. Good people. Busy as bees, involved, hard working people. Who once were so in love with Jesus that they were good dancers. Through the dance steps — Bible reading, serving, worship — they were spending time with him, and they loved it! Because they loved him.

But their love faded. And all they remembered when they passed the faith on to you were the steps that had once held so much meaning for them: "Go to church and read the Word! And one! And two! And three!"

And so you do the steps and you know they're important and you wonder why they are not really doing much for you. And now you are thinking of just quitting the Christian dance altogether. It's not working.

Just to be clear: Jesus is not saying, "Don't dance." He is saying, "Those are just the *steps* to the dance. But they're not the *point* of the dance. The point is to be with the one who loves you!"

When you understand that, the dance is energizing and exciting again. The steps feel totally different when you are in love.

So how do you get back to that first love? Jesus gets to that next.

☰ APPLY IT

Have you ever found that your busyness is distracting you from your first love for Christ? Do you feel that way now?

6

REKINDLING THE FIRE

In the previous chapter I shared an email from a college student. About a year later he wrote,

> I can't really pinpoint where the burned out attitude started. Serving God became so much of a duty that I honestly gave it up. I remember feeling lax. Stale.
>
> Then I remembered from a Bible study a couple years ago the verse, "Taste and see that the Lord is good." And I remembered the good taste. In the midst of my situation, I remembered what it was like to love the Lord. And I missed it. Then I found a book called *The Sacred Romance*. The subtitle intrigued me: *Drawing Closer to the Heart of God*.
>
> I started to realize some stuff. I was living out of duty, service, obligation. And I had completely forgotten that God, the creator of all things, chose to win back our *hearts*. He stepped down from his throne, died and rose again, for my *heart*. He wanted my *heart*, and wanted it to be totally captivated by what He did for me. That is what is life-changing.
>
> Now my time in the Word is exciting, my prayer life is honest, loud, and heartfelt. I still stumble, but now when I

look up I see a smiling face, and a hand reaching down to say, "I love you, and I am delighted to help you."

How can you recover your own first love like that? Jesus mentions three aspects to this, the same three things that young man described in his email:

> *"Consider how far you have fallen! Repent and do the things you did at first."* REV. 2:5A NIV

In that one short verse, Jesus has the prescription:

REMEMBER

He tells the Ephesians to remember the height from which they have fallen. How does this help?

Try it. Try it right now. Remember what it was like the first time you felt you were in love? Remember how, when you were talking on the phone, no one wanted to hang up... Ever? Remember giving little gifts? Or remember the first time you felt your imagination captured by anything: Listening to music, swinging a bat, playing an instrument, drawing a picture?

Just as the college student "remembered what it was like to love the Lord," it's good to remember these high points of our lives. In fact, marriage counselors say it's an exercise that almost never fails to help struggling spouses.

So remember. Remember when you would pray and sing and study because you loved Jesus, not because it was your duty.

REPENT

This word "repent" is so misunderstood. It's the Greek word *metanoia*, which means to change your mind, to change the direction of your thinking.

If you view your spiritual life as a scorecard, and getting straight A's on your spiritual progress report is the goal of the Christian life, then you're going to get real busy and lose your first love.

But if you change your thinking — if you see it as a relationship — then you'll want to spend time with the one who loves you.

REDO

Do the things you used to do, Jesus instructs. Like they say, it's easier to act your way into a feeling than to feel your way into an action.

Take marriage. You feel your first love for your spouse slipping away. You don't think, "That's it. The marriage is over!" (at least I hope you don't!). No, if you're wise, you say, "I am going to go on a date with my spouse and plan a getaway and write little notes — because I know if I do, I will get that spark back!"

That's what Jesus is saying here: Let's hang out together again.

CONFUSING THE GOSPEL

The problem with the Ephesian Christians was that they were confusing the *response* to the gospel with the *gospel*. They were doing good works, they were enduring, they were patient, were watching their doctrine. But those things are all a *response* to the gospel. They are not the gospel. And churches get this mixed up all the time. The gospel is that God is holy and we are not, and he loves us so much that he took care of that problem by sending God the Son, who died and rose again to bring us to him. When I respond to that, when his love captures my heart, I want to give, to share, to study, to endure.

Matt Chandler, in his book *The Explicit Gospel*, puts it this way: "If we confuse the gospel with response to the gospel, we will drift from what keeps the gospel on the ground... and the next thing you know we will be doing a bunch of things that obscure the gospel, not reveal it. At the end of the day, our central hope is not that all the poor will be fed, but that Jesus is Lord." [6]

That's what happened to the Christians at Ephesus. They had the actions. But they had forgotten the love that inspired those actions in the first place. The good news: It is possible for that love to be rekindled.

The early American preacher Jonathan Edwards wrote of his own return to first love:

> I was very concerned about the things of religion... and was abundant in duties. I used to pray five times a day in secret ... it was my delight to abound in religious duties. [Then one day I] was reading I Tim. 1:17. As I read, there came into my soul, and was as it were diffused through it, a sense of the glory of the Divine Being; a new sense, quite different from any thing I ever experienced before... I thought with myself, how happy I should be, if I might enjoy that God, and be rapt up to him in heaven, and be, as it were, swallowed up in him for ever! I kept singing over these words of scripture to myself; and went to pray to God that I might enjoy him, and prayed in a manner quite different from what I used to do; with affection. [7]

≡ APPLY IT

Consider your own spiritual condition. Do you sometimes get so busy for God that you forget the relationship with God? Pray that God will help you remember, repent (change your thinking) and redo what you did at first.

---

6   Matt Chandler with Jared Wilson, *The Explicit Gospel*, Wheaton: Crossway, 2012, p. 85

7   Jonathan Edwards, *The Works of Jonathan Edwards*, London: William Ball, 1839, page iv

DIGGING DEEPER

Our culture is sports-crazy, but the first century world of the New Testament would have given us a run for the money.

Six of the seven cities in this section of Revelation, all but Thyatira, had huge stadiums and regularly hosted major sporting events. The athletes would compete in footraces, wrestling, boxing, discus, javelin, long jump, chariot racing, poetry reading and singing (you read that right).

It might interest modern readers to know that, according to several inscriptions from New Testament times, women occasionally competed in these games too. And not just in poetry and singing. Descriptions of the Isthmian games near Corinth during the first century mention women winning the 200-meter dash as well as the war chariot races. [8]

The Greek Goddess of victory, Nike, in the ruins of Ephesus. She is holding out the "Victor's Crown," an olive wreath given to sports champions.

8   http://www.biblearchaeology.org/post/2012/07/16/Going-for-the-Gold-The-Apostle-Paul-and-the-Isthmian-Games.aspx#Article

7

THE ETERNAL PRIZE

"Whoever has ears, let them hear what the Spirit says to the churches. To the one who is victorious, I will give the right to eat from the tree of life, which is in the paradise of God." REV. 2:7 NIV

E ach of the seven messages ends with what scholars call a "victor saying," a promise from Jesus that a reward will go to the "one who is victorious."

These sayings all use the verb form of the Greek word *nike*, which means "victory" or "triumph." Of course, in our culture we know the word because of the athletic shoe company, but in ancient Greece, Nike was the name of the goddess of victory.

As I continued exploring the ruins of Ephesus, I saw a relief sculpture of Nike, with a palm branch in one hand and a wreath in the other. In Greek culture the palm branch signified triumph, and the wreath was worn like a crown by sports champions.

You often won a few other benefits too. Sometimes your debts were forgiven, and you were invited to a banquet with the local ruler. At other times the prize was a lifetime exemption from taxes or a lifetime invitation to dine with the ruler.

But in the Book of Revelation, it's as if Jesus keeps trumping imagery used in first-century culture. Nike gives measly olive wreaths to the victors? Well, I give the crown of life — eternal life! Athletes win the right to eat a meal with the ruler? Well, I will give the right to eat from the tree of life in paradise!

TREE OF REFUGE

The "tree of life," like many of the images so skillfully employed in these seven letters, had symbolic associations for both Jewish and Greek cultures.

For the Jews, the tree of life was a reminder of paradise, the Garden of Eden, where people enjoyed an unbroken relationship with God.

For the Ephesians, the term "tree of life" also had a fascinating local meaning. The famed Temple of Artemis was built around a sacred tree shrine. From ancient times, this tree was a place of refuge. If you were accused of a crime, but could get to the tree, you were safe. The tree literally saved your life. [9]

Do you see the layers of meaning this must have had for the Ephesians? It's like three-dimensional poetry. Jesus says these Ephesian Christians will find refuge, made possible by his death on the "tree" of the cross, at the tree of life in the restored paradise, the new heaven and new earth. As he does again and again in *The Seven*, Jesus is redeeming and enriching a local pagan symbol with Christian meaning.

The point is this: It's an amazing prize! You can sacrifice your life for a prize that will soon wither like a crown of leaves, or for a reward that will never end.

≡ APPLY IT

What are you giving your life for? What reward are you working toward?

9   Colin J Hemer, *The Letters of the Seven Church of Asia in their Local Settings*, Grand Rapids: Eerdman's. p. 42-49

DIGGING DEEPER

"If you don't repent, I will come and remove your lampstand from its place among the churches." REV. 2:5

What does Jesus mean by *"remove your lampstand"*? Remember that the "lampstands" are identified as the local churches in Rev. 1:20. So it must mean that if the churches do not respond to Christ's call to repent, he will remove them from their position of influence. He will shut down that local church.

Of course, not every local church that closes does so as a result of Christ's discipline. But many churches that were once great, influential congregations have literally shut down when abusive leadership was exposed, or doctrinal compromise weakened the body. I think this is evidence that Jesus is still involved with the church, and longs for it to be healthy and to reflect his personality. He wants church reform even more than any of the church's earthly critics. Sometimes churches that have gone askew stay alive for a while, but that's evidence of Jesus' patience and love, not necessarily his approval (as we'll see when we look at Thyatira later).

Did Christ's call to repentance have an impact on the Ephesian church? Well, it remained a healthy and influential Christian community for many centuries.

Two decades after this letter, the church at Ephesus was still important enough to be addressed in a letter written by Bishop Ignatius of Antioch that begins, "…to the Church which is at Ephesus, in Asia, deservedly most happy, being blessed in the greatness and fullness of God the Father.…"

I love how he points out a wonderful personality trait of this church. They were known for being happy. I think this is evidence the Ephesians heard and responded to the message of Christ. They did return to their first love! And at great personal risk, the Christians at Ephesus supported Ignatius, who was taken to Rome for execution.

Ephesus was also the setting for an ecumenical council of all the Christian churches in the world in 431, again showing it was one of the leading churches in the world at the time. So they flourished for many more centuries. They heard and applied what Jesus said. How about you?

First floor of ancient three-story agora of Smyrna

THE SECOND LETTER

8

THE AROMA OF LIFE

Our Turkish guide leads me down a narrow alley that does not look very promising. Old billboards cling to a chain link fence lining one side of the alley, while brick tenements stand seemingly derelict on the other.

But then we go through a tiny gate, and I walk into a hive of activity, a busy archaeological site. Workmen push wheelbarrows, field directors shout orders, an entire crew stands on scaffolding brushing mud away from the side of an ancient archway. They are uncovering the remarkable remains of the largest covered marketplace ever discovered from the Roman era. These are the ruins of Smyrna.

The main archaeological site was a three-story *agora*, or marketplace, the size of a football field, resembling our indoor malls today. As scholars here slowly peel away the debris of centuries, they are revealing two floors of the marketplace that still stand much as they did in Roman times. Shop names, fountains, and even precious merchandise are coming to light after centuries underground.

It's fitting that the only extensive ruins visitors can see here are the remains of the ancient marketplace. Smyrna was a very successful commercial port on the Aegean Sea.[10]

---

10 I owe my description of the origins of Smyrna's name to Dr. Charles Dyer, *"The Land and The Book"* podcast, January 17, 2015

CITY OF FRAGRANCE

The origin of the name of the city, "Smyrna," is shrouded in mystery. Some believe it was named after a mythological female Amazon warrior. The Greek word is also the name of an aromatic resin harvested from trees that grow in the Arabian peninsula and in some parts of Africa. You know it by its English name, "myrrh."

Myrrh was highly prized and extremely valuable. It was a key ingredient for incense, and was also used in perfume and medicine. No one knows how this city came to have the same name as this valued spice, but it's a good bet that somewhere in the ruins of the marketplace there were shops selling myrrh. Perhaps Smyrna was the main point of connection for Greco-Roman merchants to the far-off and exotic myrrh harvesters.

As Bible scholar Dr. Charles Dyer points out, myrrh was such a powerful, attractive scent that it was used to embalm the dead. It made the smell of decay, disease, and death more bearable. Its pungent aroma hid all those other smells.

Dr. Dyer says he sees an association between the church at Smyrna and that aromatic spice. The church at Smyrna was very familiar with suffering and death. Yet the way the church endured all that tragedy was to stay focused on the sweet fragrance of the Savior.

THE AROMA OF CHRIST

Jesus offered hope and comfort to this church that was facing incredible suffering and persecution. There are no words of condemnation in this letter, only commendation. Jesus says to them, in effect: Death will come, but remember, I have conquered death and so can offer eternal life. Don't be afraid. Be faithful.

"To the angel of the church in Smyrna write:

*"These are the words of him who is the First and the Last, who
died and came to life again. I know your afflictions and your
poverty — yet you are rich! I know about the slander of those who
say they are Jews and are not, but are a synagogue of Satan. Do
not be afraid of what you are about to suffer. I tell you, the devil
will put some of you in prison to test you, and you will suffer
persecution for ten days. Be faithful, even to the point of death,
and I will give you life as your victor's crown.*

*"Whoever has ears, let them hear what the Spirit says to the
churches. The one who is victorious will not be hurt at all by the
second death."* REV. 2:8-11 NIV

People who suffer, who feel blown away by tragedy, wrestle not only
with the question "Why?" but also with the question "Who?" Who is
God, that he would allow suffering?

Jesus answers this question. God himself came to earth and suffered
and died. When I suffer, he is right there with me, sympathizing
because he suffered too. Then he reminds us that though he died, he
lives again. And so will we!

THE BEST IS YET TO COME

And Jesus' reminder of his own death and resurrection puts the coming
suffering and death of many in the church at Smyrna in perspective.

Beloved Bible scholar Dr. Howard Hendricks once said:

> The amazing thing is not that we die. The amazing thing is
> that we live! We think we are in the land of the living on our
> way to the land of the dying. Nothing could be further from
> the truth. We are in the land of the dying on our way to the
> land of the living! [11]

---

11 Quoted in Richard F. Brumme, *The Walking Wounded*. iUniverse, 2006. p.2

Jesus' words to the church at Smyrna are a reminder to keep all the good and bad stuff of life in perspective. The best is yet to come! And while we wait, and bad things in life happen in this broken world, the aroma of Jesus and his promise of resurrection can help us endure.

☰ APPLY IT

What situations are you facing related to death and suffering?

How does it help to remember that Jesus promises a resurrection and restoration, and ultimate victory?

9

CULTURE SHIFT

Smyrna is one of the oldest continuously inhabited cities in the world; there's been a city here for over 8,000 years! Why? It has a perfect, mild climate. It has an ideal location, right on the west coast of Asia Minor where the Hermes River runs into the Aegean Sea. Trade routes have funneled merchants through the valley to the well-protected harbor for longer than recorded history.

The Greek historian Strabo called it "the most beautiful of all cities" and specifically praised its excellent street plan. The Golden Street, connecting the temples of Zeus and Cybele, is said to have been the finest street in antiquity. [12]

Today it's the modern city of Izmir (a version of the word "Smyrna") in Turkey. It's a beautiful, large city right on the coast, which makes archaeology difficult because there's a modern settlement over most of the area, and people object to having their homes dug up to reveal ruins underneath! But the ancient marketplace was hidden under a cemetery, preserving it from modern construction that might have destroyed the remains. While the ruins were discovered beneath the cemetery during World War II, detailed excavation only began in

---

12 Descriptions of ancient Smyrna from http://www.welcometohosanna.com/REVELATION/Smyrna. html, accessed April 2015

1996. I enjoyed watching archaeologists digging up artifacts that will be exhibited to tourists in future years.

ALL HAIL CAESAR?

Eager to demonstrate its loyalty to Rome when the Romans expanded into Asia Minor in 133 BC, Smyrna built a temple to the goddess Roma (the patron deity of Rome). The city never wavered in its allegiance to Rome, and so the emperors always protected it and generously financed its development.

In 26 AD Smyrna won out over other area cities for the honor of building a temple to the Roman emperor Tiberius, and from then on it became a center for emperor worship.

Every year under the rule of Domitian, the residents would join a parade to the emperor's temple and throw a pinch of incense into the sacrificial fire there while proclaiming, "Caesar is Lord and God."

Most saw it as a harmless but politically important gesture ensuring continued support from the volatile Caesar. But the Christians saw it as heresy. There was only one Lord, and only one God, and he sure wasn't a paranoid politician.

So they usually refused. And this meant huge pressure, resentment, and persecution against them from the rest of the city. The way the other residents saw it, Christians were endangering not just their own lives, but the status of the city itself as the capital of emperor worship!

FAMILY TENSION

Interestingly, there was just one escape from the requirement to worship Caesar. You had to be a Jew. For decades, Jews had been living under a carefully negotiated treaty that exempted them from worshipping Caesar. The treaty recognized that for their religion, idol worship was wrong. So instead they found other ways to show their allegiance, like donations to the city in Caesar's name.

Remember, this was very early in the history of Christianity. Until this point, the Jesus movement had been considered a kind of subset of Judaism. That's how many early Christians were able to sidestep the requirements of emperor worship. Christians were seen as a part of the Jewish religion.

But then Gentiles began to outnumber ethnic Jews in the Christian movement. They too claimed the Jewish exemption in order to get out of Caesar worship. The number of residents claiming an exemption from the emperor pledge started to climb as Christian churches grew. Local authorities began to suspect them. Were they really Jews, or just Greeks trying to get out of the requirement?

Some of the Jews in the synagogue at Smyrna became angry and afraid. The Greek Christians were not really Jews, they argued. They had not been circumcised, for example, and they didn't keep all the kosher laws. They had never converted to Judaism; they were only followers of this alleged Messiah, Jesus.

They feared that if the Romans became upset that these Greeks were using the synagogue to escape emperor worship, then the official exemption of all Jews might be at risk. So that began a process by the synagogue leaders of expelling Christians from their congregations. Of course, the Christian position at the time was that they were indeed true Jews – since they worshipped the Jewish Messiah.

This is why there was such tension between the Christians and the synagogue leaders in Smyrna. Sadly, and unnecessarily, friction between Christians and Jews has erupted at times in the centuries since this rift into the ugly shame of anti-Semitism. That is a horrific blot on church history for which there is no excuse. I pray for peace between Christians and Jews all over the world.

REJECTION BEFORE ME, REJECTION BEHIND ME

Even today, cultures can rapidly shift in regard to their opinions of religious believers, with drastic consequences. The Christians at Smyrna must have felt they were experiencing rejection from every side, the Jews and the Romans. Can you imagine how head-spinning all these developments were for the Christians? Suddenly people in their own city, which they loved, and people in their own adopted synagogue, which they also loved, considered them *persona non grata.*

Roman persecution against Christians no longer under the Jewish exemption was severe. Once they were kicked out of the synagogue and still refused to worship the emperor, the city leaders felt they needed to passionately demonstrate to Caesar that these Christians were not representative of Smyrna.

Some of them were thrown to lions to be eaten. Others were burned at the stake. Still more were covered in bloody skins of wild animals and thrown to dogs for the entertainment of the citizenry. Some were crucified. Others were simply stabbed or beheaded.

And all that is just beginning as Jesus addresses the Christians in Smyrna:

> *"To the angel of the church in Smyrna write: These are the words of him who is the First and the Last, who died and came to life again."* REV. 2:8 NIV

THE FIRST AND LAST

Each of the times in these letters when Jesus is identified, he is identified in unique terms, most of them drawn out of the vision of the glorified Christ we saw in chapter 1.

For example, here he is "The First and the Last." You first saw that in Rev. 1:17, 18. Remember how we learned that apocalyptic literature is stuffed with references to older apocalyptic writing? Well, this phrase is in Isaiah 41:4, 43:10, 44:6, and 48:12. In all those places God refers to *himself* as *"The First and the Last,"* and here it is used again to describe Jesus.

This was huge. For Smyrnan Christians threatened by a Caesar claiming to be God, Jesus reminds them that there is only one, first, last, and true God. And it's Jesus.

He is the first, meaning he preexisted, and he is the last, meaning he will go on forever. When all things begin, he is already there. When other things cease, he does not. He is the eternal infinite God. The idea is that he transcends time, he transcends space, he transcends all of creation, every human government, every achievement, every threat.

For Christians who were suddenly suffering persecution in a rapidly shifting society, imagine how comforting it was to be reminded that they served the One Lord who never changes!

We live in a rapidly changing era too. It's good to remember that our roots are deep when we abide in Jesus. He always will be, and always was. He will never change. He is our rock.

☰ APPLY IT

In what ways are you experiencing the disorienting effect of change in your own life?

How do you see our culture's opinions of Christians changing?

How can this description of Jesus give you serenity in the midst of change?

DIGGING DEEPER

Throughout the Book of Revelation, the visions predict great future persecutions against Christians.

So what was immediately ahead for the Christians in Asia Minor? Persecutions from the Roman government waxed and waned for the next two centuries. Then this area was particularly hard hit during the severe persecutions instituted by the co-emperors Diocletian and Galerius. It started in 299, when the emperors went to a pagan temple and asked the priests there to predict the future for them. The priests claimed they were unable to do so because Christians were beginning to infiltrate all of Roman society, including the emperors' own households.

So the emperors ordered all members of the court to perform a pagan sacrifice. They also sent letters to the military command, demanding the entire army perform the required sacrifices or face expulsion. Some Christians gave in, but many refused to compromise. So the persecution worsened. In the autumn of 302, Diocletian ordered that the Christian pastor of Caesarea, Romanus, have his tongue removed for defying the order. Romanus was then sent to prison, where he was executed on November 17, 303.

After this, Galerius pushed for extermination of all Christians. On February 23, 303, Diocletian ordered that the newly built church at Nicomedia be torn down, its Bibles burned, and its treasures stolen. The next day, his first "Edict against the Christians" was published. It ordered the destruction of all Christian scriptures and places of worship across the empire, and prohibited Christians from meeting for worship. Executions of many Christians followed. One man, Peter Cubicularius, was stripped and scourged, salt and vinegar were poured in his wounds, and he was slowly roasted over an open fire. Other Christians were publicly decapitated. Diocletian then ordered the arrest of all the Christian clergy and required universal acts of sacrifice to the Roman gods.

However, even this intense persecution was unsuccessful. It created sympathy for Christians among the pagan Romans and inspired the rest of the believers. The emperors finally rescinded the edict in 311, announcing that the persecution had failed to bring Christians back to traditional religion. The attempt to eradicate all Christians had lasted less than eight years. Within twenty-five years of what would come to be called the Great Persecution, the emperor Constantine attempted to reverse the consequences of the edicts, making reparations and returning all confiscated property to Christians.

This turn of events is exactly the pattern predicted by the Book of Revelation: There will be times of great persecution, but they will never last, and ultimately Christians will prosper; if not here on earth, then when they reign with Christ in glory. So, the point is, don't give in, and don't give up; instead, look up!

The story of persecution is not just ancient history. There's persecution ahead, too. More Christians are in mortal danger for practicing their faith now than ever in history. We need to pray for our brothers and sisters, particularly those in the Middle East. And we need to be prepared to endure opposition with grace, faith, and love.

Ruins of the Temple of Hadrian in Ephesus. A statue base with an inscription belonging to Diocletian was later added.
Both emperors persecuted Christians severely.

10

YOU CAN'T KEEP
A GOOD MAN DOWN

A mazingly, this same One we saw yesterday who is the First and Last, who is eternal, who was before all things and will live forever, says that he *died*. He can relate to the fate facing the Christians at Smyrna. But it gets better: He was also raised to life!

> *"These are the words of him ...who died and came to life again."*
>
> REV. 2:8 NIV

It's the most basic Christian belief: Jesus is God eternal (The First and Last), entering into our history for the very purpose of dying. But he rose again. That is the heart of the gospel.

I've noticed that only in countries where there is little persecution of Christians are there churches that try to deny the physical, literal resurrection of Jesus. Life is good for people in countries without a lot of persecution, so perhaps many there feel it's enough to see Jesus as a good teacher who died thousands of years ago. In most of the rest of the world, where Christians carry social stigma and are often persecuted, the resurrection is always affirmed by those daring to call themselves Christ-followers. It's only in this truth that there is lasting hope.

How does the resurrection bring hope?

IT VALIDATES CHRIST'S CLAIMS

The resurrection is proof that Jesus is who he claimed to be – the Messiah. If Jesus had remained dead, he would have been just another religious martyr. But when God raised Jesus from the dead, it was evidence that Jesus was telling the truth. [13]

IT ASSURES ME OF MY OWN RESURRECTION

The resurrection gives me hope that the God who raised Jesus to life again will do the same for everyone who believes in Jesus. People long for immortality like thirsty people long for water – and that longing can be fulfilled! Imagine the hope this gave the persecuted Christians in Smyrna who must have felt they were like candles soon to be snuffed out.

IT ASSURES ME CHRIST IS LIVING AND WITH ME

Phillips Brooks was a beloved pastor and songwriter. Outside Trinity Episcopal Church in Boston today there's a life-sized statue of the preacher. On its base are the words: "Phillips Brooks – Preacher of the Word of God – Lover of Mankind." The statue depicts Brooks standing next to his pulpit. It's a nice statue of a former pastor. But it's not really about him: Towering above Phillips Brooks is the living Christ with his right hand resting on Brooks' shoulder.

Of course, as a pastor, I love that! The resurrection of Jesus means he is really alive and supportive and aware of whatever I am going through. Again, think of the electric surge of confidence the Smyrna Christians must have felt when they heard a letter from this living Jesus – alive and active after death – which they themselves are now facing!

---

13 Read more about all three points at http://www.christianpost.com/news/seven-assurances-the-resurrection-gives-92915

≡ **APPLY IT**

How does the resurrection of Jesus give you hope?

Why is the resurrection a crucial Christian belief?

11

HE KNOWS

Suffering is a fact of life. No one gets to choose whether or not they suffer. Everyone does, in one way or another.

The only thing you get to choose is how you'll respond to suffering. And not only how you'll respond to *your own* suffering. Maybe you are grieved at the suffering of a loved one, or the suffering of people around the world. Those thoughts can be overwhelming at times.

Jesus has a message for you.

> *"I know your afflictions and your poverty — yet you are rich! I know about the slander of those who say they are Jews and are not, but are a synagogue of Satan."* REV. 2:9 NIV

First, some hugely important historical context. Of course this reference to "a synagogue of Satan" was not an attack against Jews in general, but a reference to those in the Smyrna synagogue who denounced the Christians before Roman officials for not being "true Jews." As we learned earlier this week, these Christians were being expelled from the synagogue, leaving them open to persecution. Jews were exempt from participation in the cult of emperor worship, but if the Christians were expelled from the synagogue, they did not enjoy the same legal protection.

In his message to Smyrna, Jesus gives some encouraging affirmations that you could summarize in two words each.

I KNOW

First, he says, *"I know..."* He knows what? It's as if he lists an ascending scale of troubles.

"I know your afflictions..." The Greek word translated "afflictions" means "distresses." It's a picture of unending, crushing pressure. Maybe you can identify with that right now.

"I know... your poverty..." Unlike the Christians in Ephesus or Laodicea or other cities where they could be found in the upper middle classes, the Christians here in Smyrna were poor. Probably even employing people who would not show allegiance to the emperor was seen as an unacceptable risk, so it was difficult for them to find work.

"I know... the slander..." There was a smear campaign going on against these believers. It didn't stop with the simple truth of their allegiance to Jesus. It went on into lies and innuendo. For example, we know from early writers that, because Christians talked about eating and drinking the body and blood of Jesus, some Romans accused them of cannibalism!

And Jesus says about all these struggles, *"I know."* And it's what he says to you and me today.

Every single thing you are going through in life. He sees it all.

Tom Holladay puts it this way: "Here are some phrases that will never come out of Christ's mouth: 'I didn't see that coming!' 'Total shock to me!' 'You've *got* to be kidding!' 'Run that by me again?'" Why? Because Jesus, who is God, knows absolutely everything, and that includes everything you're going through in your life right now.

You're not going through it alone. You may feel alone, you may feel like no one knows and no one understands but he knows what you're going through. Every detail of it. In fact, he knows more about it than you do. [14]

HE UNDERSTANDS

But when Jesus says, "I know" again and again to the Christians in Smyrna, he doesn't just mean he is aware. He is saying, "I know" in the sense of "I understand."

He understands what it's like to be afflicted, because he was afflicted. He understands what it's like to be slandered, because he was slandered. He understands what it's like to live in poverty, because he didn't have a place to call his own. He understands betrayal, ridicule, and rejection. He even understands death. Whatever you are going through, he has been through already. And he is with you every step of the way.

You may feel like no one knows, and no one understands, but he does. Every detail of it.

≡ APPLY IT

How does it encourage you to hear Jesus say, "I know" and "I understand"?

---

14 From *"What Jesus Says to a Suffering Church"*, sermon preached by Tom Holladay at Saddleback Church, Orange County, accessed at saddlebackresources.com

12

DO NOT ENTERTAIN FEAR

Earlier this year I was in Zambia, Africa, visiting a very remote village. While there I interviewed a pastor named Rex who is going into an even more remote area to take over as pastor at a church there. The man he is replacing, Crispin, was murdered.

Villagers who felt Christianity threatened their traditional religion told Crispin they were cursing him, and that the gods of the village would take his life. Crispin told them he was not afraid. My friends found Crispin's body a few weeks later in a lake nearby, murdered with a hatchet.

I asked Rex how he found the strength to go into such a hostile situation. He spoke of confidence in the grace of God, grace that surges and strengthens us when we are thrust into unusual situations. Then he said words I'll never forget: "As Christians, we must refuse to entertain fear."

Do you ever "entertain fear"? Treat it like a guest in your brain? Welcome it in, serve it drinks, feed it snacks, invite it to stay a while, listen to its stories?

We live in a culture that has figured out that fear gets our attention. That's why so much of what passes for entertainment in our society is fear-based. Radio talk shows are fear-based, the news is fear-based, Hollywood movies are fear-based. But Jesus tells the Christians at Smyrna, who, it would seem, had every reason to fear, not to entertain such thoughts.

> *"Do not be afraid of what you are about to suffer. I tell you, the devil will put some of you in prison to test you, and you will suffer persecution for ten days. Be faithful, even to the point of death, and I will give you life as your victor's crown."* REV. 2:10 NIV

FEAR NOT

"Do not be afraid" — or *"Fear not"* as it's translated in some Bibles — is another of those two-word affirmations from Jesus in this letter. This is one of the most common phrases in the Bible. Eighty-three times we are told in Scripture, "Fear not."

Ok... so how do we pull that off? I sometimes wake up with nightmares. I get sweaty palms when I see a needle. We all have things that make us afraid. The National Institute of Health says that phobias — fears — are the most common psychological problems in America. So how do you follow this advice to "fear not"?

Well, first, notice Jesus does not say, "Do not feel." He says, "Do not fear."

Some belief systems teach that the way to deal with suffering and fear is to simply detach from any deep emotional ties. As that great spiritual master Yoda said in the Star Wars movies, "Attachment is the path to the dark side. Let go of all you fear to lose." It's only a movie, but that is one solution a lot of people try.

But Jesus loved people with passion. He cried over the lostness of the city of Jerusalem with passion. He wept loudly when his good friend Lazarus died. Detachment is not Jesus' way out of fear. It's not about the absence of feeling. It's about the presence of peace.

Also note that Jesus does not say, "Fear not... for you will not suffer."

Some Christians think we should affirm that no bad thing will ever happen – no cancer, no disease, no suffering. And if bad things happen to you, well then, you just did not have enough faith.

No. In fact Jesus very specifically says, "You will suffer persecution for ten days."

NOT ELEVEN

Remember, the Book of Revelation uses numbers in symbolic ways. He's probably not saying they're only going to be in prison for a week and a half. Ten days is an expression for a limited period of time. The point is, it has an end. It's not eleven days. It's ten.

Jesus also says the same to us. You and I will go through hard times. He says in the Gospel of John, "In this world you will have trouble..." (JOHN 16:33). That's a promise you'll never find in one of those Bible pocket promise books they sell at the grocery store! But you've got his word on it: You'll have trouble. If you expect that God owes you a life without trouble, you're in for a big surprise. And when that surprise comes, some Christians walk away from God, thinking he let them down.

But not if you hear what he says to the churches.

"Do not be afraid of what you are about to suffer..."

Jesus is telling you how to live in the real world when he says this. Fake-world Jesus would say, "Do not be afraid. You don't have anything hard ahead of you. Life will be perfect." But here's the real-world truth: You are going to go through tough times. Every one of us does. I guarantee you, in heaven, every one of us will have a tale to tell!

But take the time you suffer on earth, put it next to eternity, and it's like – ten days. It's a short time. So don't quit.

Sports doctors have analyzed the tenacity of the best marathon runners. Dr. Jeroen Swart, who works for the Sports Science Institute of South Africa, concludes, "Some think elite athletes have an easy time of it," but that's a wrong assumption. "It never gets easier... You hurt just as much." Accepting the reality of pervasive pain, he explains, leads to more realistic expectations and faster times: "Knowing how to accept [the reality of the pain] allows people to improve their performance." [15]

I think that's why Jesus is honest with these Christians. There will be suffering. There will be pain. But knowing how to accept the reality of the pain helps.

And he guarantees a reward after their trials. *"A victor's crown."* That was the garland of leaves placed on the head of the victor of a competition, or a special person the city chose to honor. Smyrna was particularly well known for this tradition. A long series of inscriptions found there describes the wreath of victory given as a crown to various citizens. But Jesus says he will give *"life... as your victor's crown."* He won't just give some crown of leaves. He'll give a crown of life — eternal life!

Maybe you are facing grief, unanswered prayer, loneliness, broken dreams. Jesus is not saying to pretend that suffering doesn't hurt. Because it does. He is not saying that life isn't hard. Because it is. He is saying, "Trust me."

He promises your suffering will one day end. And he will restore all things to the perfection God intended from the first, and reward you with abundant life!

≡ APPLY IT

What hardships are you facing? What do you fear? How can the words of the living Jesus encourage you?

---

15   Quoted in Samuel R. Chand, *"The Power of Tenacity"*, on Leadership Network web site, accessed at http://leadnet.org/the-power-of-tenacity/

13

COURAGE IN THE FIRE

So did the words of Jesus to the Christians at Smyrna have effect? Did the Christians here stand up to persecution or did they give up and compromise?

A famous man named Polycarp was the pastor of the church at Smyrna about fifty years after this letter was written. Very likely he heard this letter read when he was in his thirties and the Book of Revelation came to Smyrna for the very first time.

When Polycarp was about 86 years old, the Roman government's representative in Smyrna, known as the proconsul, got word to start another persecution of Christians in order to wipe them out. He apparently thought, *Let's go right to the top. If we get the old pastor Polycarp to deny Christ, the whole thing might crumble.*

And so on February 22, 156 AD, guards were sent to arrest Polycarp. They went to his house, where Polycarp insisted they first join him for some lunch. He fed them, and then asked to pray for them. They nervously agreed, and he proceeded to ask God's blessing on them for the next two hours! Finally they interrupted him, told him they had to go, and he was brought under escort to an arena in the middle of the city.

Picture the scene. The crowds are calling for his blood. Remember, the proconsul's goal is to elicit a public denial of Christ, not to kill him. So he says first, "Think of your age. Just say, 'Caesar is Lord.'" Polycarp refuses.

So the proconsul says, "How about just saying, 'Away with the atheists!'" Christians were called "atheists" by the Romans because they worshipped an invisible God with no physical temple. Polycarp agrees, waves his arms to the bloodthirsty crowds, and says, "Away with the atheists!"

Finally the proconsul begs Polycarp, "I will set you free if you reproach Christ!"

And what Polycarp says next becomes famous. He looks the Roman representative right in the eye and says, "Eighty and six years have I served him, and he has done me no wrong. How can I now blaspheme my King, who saved me?"

The proconsul tries one last time: "I will burn you alive if you don't change your mind!"

But Polycarp answers,

> You threaten me with fire which burns for an hour and then is extinguished. But you are ignorant of the fire of coming judgment. So what are you waiting for? I will not change my mind, so do what you will.

Those who were there said Polycarp spoke with such confidence and joy, and his face was so full of grace, that he didn't seem troubled in the least by the things said to him.

So the Romans put a stake in the ground and surrounded it with dry wood. Just before they lit the woodpile they tried nailing Polycarp to the wooden stake so he wouldn't be able to run away from the fire, but he said, "Leave me as I am; he that gives me strength to endure the fire will also enable me to stay here, without your pitiful safeguard of nails."

And that's how he died.[16]

THE EFFECT OF HOPE

The Roman proconsul's plan badly misfired. News of Polycarp's composure spread instantly throughout the world, he was widely quoted among both Christians and pagans, and his example galvanized the courage of the churches and raised the sympathies of the Romans — exactly the opposite effect Caesar wanted.

Polycarp heard and believed Jesus' words,

> *"Be faithful, even to the point of death, and I will give you life as your victor's crown."* REV. 2:10B NLT

You may be thinking, "I could never be faithful to the point of death like that!"

You know what I've discovered? God doesn't give me the strength to face problems I don't have. He just gives me the strength to face problems I do have. If I will receive it.

Many people have told me, "I was so afraid of what might happen if I ever lost my spouse... lost my job... got cancer... but then it happened. And God is giving me strength to go through it."

I'm not saying it won't hurt. It hurts terribly. But I am saying that when it hurts, that's when God gives you strength. In that very moment.

≡ APPLY IT

Today give God your fears and ask him for the reassurance that he will give you the strength you need in the moment you need it.

---

16 The Martyrdom of Polycarp, translated by J. B. Lightfoot, edited for the web by Dan Graves, accessed at http://www.christianhistoryinstitute.org/study/module/polycarp

14

NO NEED TO FEAR

Polycarp, whose story we heard yesterday, was not the last martyr, of course. Many experts believe Christians today are undergoing the most widespread period of persecution since Roman times.

A recent report states that Christian persecution reached historic levels in 2014, with approximately 100 million Christians around the world facing possible dire consequences for merely practicing their religion. [17]

According to Open Door, which is something like Amnesty International for persecuted believers, on average each month 322 Christians are killed for their faith. Each month 214 churches are destroyed and 772 acts of violence are committed against Christians. [18]

These are tragedies we must oppose. We all need to pray for and support our persecuted brothers and sisters. And we can also learn from them. The lives of persecuted Christians reveal that even when things look out of control, believers can rest secure, knowing that God is still in control.

---

17 http://www.religionnews.com/2015/01/07/persecution-christians-reached-historic-levels-2014-will-2015-worse/

18 https://www.opendoorsusa.org/christian-persecution/

STAND STRONG. GOD WINS

That's the overall message of the entire Book of Revelation. Ultimately, God wins. And Jesus is able to give courage, peace and even joy to stand strong through the storm. In fact, believers discover God's love in new and powerful ways even in the midst of suffering. The Open Door website has many personal testimonies from persecuted Christians affirming this.

One Chinese church leader who spent 23 years in prison says this to Christians who do not face persecution:

> I was pushed into a cell, but you have to push yourself into one. You have no time to know God. You need to build yourself a cell, so you can do for yourself what persecution did for me – simplify your life and know God. [19]

An Egyptian Christian reflected on the way he was treated when he converted to Christ:

> In great suffering you discover a different Jesus than you do in normal life... Pain and suffering bring up to the surface all the weak points of your personality. In my weakest state, I had an incredible realization that Jesus loved me even right then. [20]

We all need to hear encouragement like this, because in many countries persecution is not obvious. But prejudice against Christians is still there. Many experience it in subtle but very real ways at work or school. It can be intimidating. We must believe the last verse of Jesus' message to the Christians in Smyrna:

> *"Whoever has ears, let them hear what the Spirit says to the churches. The one who is victorious will not be hurt at all by the second death."* REV. 2:11 NIV

---

19 https://www.opendoorsusa.org/christian-persecution/

20 Ibid.

NO FEAR OF THE SECOND DEATH

What is "the second death"? In Luke 12:5 Jesus says,

> *"I tell you, my friends, do not be afraid of those who kill the body
> and after that can do no more. Fear him who, after your body has
> been killed, has authority to throw you into hell."*

What he's saying is that the second death is the one to worry about.
The first death is only physical; the second is spiritual and eternal.
But if you are resting in God's love and grace, you need not fear. Jesus
says in the next verse, *"Not one sparrow is forgotten by God... Don't be
afraid; you are worth more than many sparrows."*

But some of you are thinking — wait a minute. This is only true of the
"victorious" or, in some translations, "the overcomers." That word is
used a lot in these seven letters. Who are the victorious? Some sort of
super-Christians?

WHO ARE THE OVERCOMERS?

In another place in the Bible, this same word is used three times by
this same writer, John, the author of the book of Revelation:

> *...everyone born of God overcomes the world. This is the victory
> that has overcome the world, even our faith. Who is it that
> overcomes the world? Only he who believes that Jesus is the Son
> of God.* 1 JOHN 5:4,5 NIV

Notice the word "everyone." If you're thinking, "not me," then what
does "everyone" mean if it doesn't mean *everyone*? If you've been born
of God, you are an overcomer. No "maybe." If you believe that Jesus is
the Son of God, and put your trust in him, the Bible says you are an
overcomer. That's what *God* says about *you*. You are a conqueror. You
are victorious. So don't turn back!

Jesus is assuring the Christians at Smyrna, "No need to fear. There
will be pain for a short time, but I'll give you life." His words have

encouraged Christians in the harshest situations for centuries. Let them encourage you too.

THE PAIN WILL NOT LAST

One day several years ago I noticed that one side of my face was going numb, becoming paralyzed. I looked up from the Sunday newspaper and asked my wife, "Honey, is there something wrong with my face?"

She screamed, "You are having a stroke!" and rushed me to the hospital. After a series of tests that included brain scans and more, it turned out I hadn't had a stroke. It was Bell's palsy: The main nerve to that side of my face had been damaged. The doctors told me that in most cases it heals itself in six months to a year. It took me nearly a year, but I finally did return to normal. At times during those months, the pain as my nerves reknit was very intense.

But when the doctor gave me that diagnosis it actually lessened my pain. It gave me hope. It gave me perspective. I had some months of this, and then I would be okay.

The promise of Jesus here does the same thing for the pain of life. It lets me know: I have some months or years of this, and then I will be okay. And I don't just mean to apply this to physical pain. I mean all the pain of life, from broken hearts to broken dreams.

THE ADVANTAGE OF PERSPECTIVE

A few years ago the History Channel did a documentary on the 60th anniversary of D-Day, the invasion of Normandy that was the turning point of World War II. They interviewed two soldiers who had been there. One had been a soldier on the ground. The other had been a pilot. The ground soldier said, "I was convinced there was no way we could possibly win." The pilot said, "I was convinced there was no way we could possibly lose."

What made the difference? The pilot had the aerial perspective. And hearing Christ's promise of his second coming and his rewards to the faithful brings that kind of aerial view. Day to day, you fight the battle on the ground. But these glimpses of the promised future assure you: There is a King who will right every wrong, who is the ultimate Judge, who will be the Victor over all these battles. His triumph is assured.

So again we ask: Did his encouragement have an impact on the believers in Smyrna? Well, there is still a Christian community (that once again faces major obstacles) in Smyrna, or Izmir, today, 20 centuries later! That little church in Smyrna has survived longer than the much wealthier and larger congregations in cities like Laodicea or Ephesus. The Christians at Smyrna heard and applied what Jesus said. How about you?

≡ APPLY IT

Please take time right now to pray for your persecuted brothers and sisters in Christ around the globe. Ask God to help them have the kind of confidence he promises to the Christians at Smyrna.

Author's family at the Agora in Pergamum

15

LIVING COUNTER-CULTURALLY

We soar up the steep cliff face of the Pergamum acropolis in an aerial tram that lifts us nearly 1,000 feet above the valley floor in a matter of seconds. When we walk out of the cable car we are stunned by the gargantuan ruins of the throne of Satan. That's the eerie name Jesus gives this place, the third of *The Seven*. Let's find out why.

Pergamum is about 15 miles from the Aegean coast in a dramatic valley leading from the coast to the interior of the country. It's impossible to overstate how impressive the ancient acropolis here is to first-time visitors. The pillars and steps that remain from gigantic ancient temples are still dizzyingly tall today.

The city was founded by Lysimachus, one of the four generals who carved up the empire of Alexander the Great after Alexander's death in 323 BC. As Dr. Charles Dyer puts it, he chose Pergamum as sort of his private bank vault because of its daunting location, and stored 9,000 talents of gold here. A talent weighs about 75 pounds, so 9,000 talents of gold is 675,000 pounds. At the time of this writing, that would make his fortune worth over $11 billion! Pergamum was the Fort Knox of its day. [21]

THE PERGAMUM PROBLEM

But Pergamum soon had a problem. About 100 years before Christ, the last king of Pergamum died without an heir. In his will he bequeathed his entire empire to Rome! The government took all the money and the city soon declined in importance as Ephesus replaced it as the dominant financial power in the region.

Still, Pergamum continued as a major center of religion and learning. There was a famous medical school here dedicated to Asclepius, the Greek god of healing. The famed ancient physician Galen was from Pergamum. The city library housed 200,000 volumes, the second largest library in the ancient world next to Alexandria.

Most impressive to visitors today, massive altars and temples were built on the precipitously high cliff. The first were dedicated to Athena and Zeus. A temple to Serapis, the ancient Egyptian god of the underworld, was built in the lower city of Pergamum. Later came a center for the worship of the Roman Emperor, which dominated the skyline for miles around as it loomed over the valley from its place high on the hill.

And that temple created a major problem for the Christians living in Pergamum. How do you serve God in a city that is trying to show its devotion to Rome by worshipping the emperor as a god?

PRESSURE FROM THE INSIDE

In addition to that problem, there was an even bigger threat here — not just persecution from the outside, but also false teaching on the inside.

---

21 Much of this description of ancient Pergamum from Dr. Charles Dyer, *"The Land and The Book"* podcast, January 25, 2015

In his letter to the church at Pergamum, Jesus singles out those in the Pergamum church who were apparently trying to compromise with the prevailing culture in Pergamum, which was one of idolatry and immorality. He gives the shocking diagnosis that the disease of compromise is coming from within the church, not from outside pressure.

He says there is a teacher in the church there like the Old Testament character Balaam, who led the Israelites to commit idolatry through the temptation of sexual immorality.

And Jesus lets the Pergamum Christians know this teaching is not from him.

> *"Write this letter to the angel of the church in Pergamum. This is the message from the one with the sharp two-edged sword:*
>
> *"I know that you live in the city where Satan has his throne, yet you have remained loyal to me. You refused to deny me even when Antipas, my faithful witness, was martyred among you there in Satan's city.*
>
> *"But I have a few complaints against you. You tolerate some among you whose teaching is like that of Balaam, who showed Balak how to trip up the people of Israel. He taught them to sin by eating food offered to idols and by committing sexual sin.*
>
> *"In a similar way, you have some Nicolaitans among you who follow the same teaching. Repent of your sin, or I will come to you suddenly and fight against them with the sword of my mouth.*
>
> *"Anyone with ears to hear must listen to the Spirit and understand what he is saying to the churches. To everyone who is victorious I will give some of the manna that has been hidden away in heaven. And I will give to each one a white stone, and on the stone will be engraved a new name that no one understands except the one who receives it."* REV. 2:12-17 NLT

In some ways our culture today has parallels to the culture at Pergamum. There is unrelenting pressure for Christians to conform to a relativistic, do-your-own-thing mindset.

Christians can't expect everyone else in our culture to live according to standards found in God's Word. Yet we still are part of God's people, and are called by the One who loves us to live Christ-like, obedient lives.

That means part of being a Christ-follower is living counter-culturally. The art of the Christian life is learning how to stay counter-cultural in the ways that really matter to Jesus.

≡ APPLY IT

Do you ever feel pressure to conform to the standards of the world? In what ways?

How can you live "in the world and yet not of the world"?

16

THE ONE WITH THE SWORD

The might of the Roman Empire was represented throughout the world by the powerful governors appointed by the Senate. Their might was far greater than the power we assign to governors in the United States today.

As I mentioned earlier, a governor was given "the right of the sword" in his province. The Latin expression is *ius gladii*. This meant that the governor, and only the governor, literally had the power of life or death over his subjects (that's why the high priest Caiaphas and his conspirators could not kill Jesus, but needed to involve the Roman governor of Judea, Pontius Pilate). The governor of the Roman province of Asia had his official seat, where he wielded his official sword, in Pergamum.

I think that's why Jesus describes himself in the following way at the start of the letter to the Christians in this city:

> *"Write this letter to the angel of the church in Pergamum. This is the message from the one with the sharp two-edged sword."*
>
> REV. 2:12 NLT

Imagine how encouraging it must have been to this band of believers to be reminded that the Roman governor did not hold the ultimate power over their lives. Instead, Jesus was really the one who held the double-edged sword of justice!

Jesus says in the next verse:

> *"You refused to deny me even when Antipas, my faithful witness, was martyred among you there in Satan's city."* REV. 2:13B NLT

Antipas is the only person apart from John mentioned by name in Revelation. He was apparently a leader of the house churches in Pergamum.[22] Antipas was probably killed for refusing to acknowledge Caesar as Lord, the same reason Polycarp was later martyred.

THE FAITHFUL WITNESS

Antipas is called "my faithful witness." That's the highest praise Jesus could give anyone. Christ himself is called "the faithful witness" in Rev. 1:5. When he commends saints in heaven he'll say, "Well done, good and faithful servant." So faithfulness is important to Jesus.

But what does it mean to stay faithful? Not to be sinless — no one is. It means to develop consistency, to persevere in your Christian witness despite all the distractions and temptations.

That will mean being counter-cultural when the culture is asking you to deny or compromise your faith in Jesus.

And I'm not just talking about secular culture. Christian culture, too, can drift from the central message of Jesus. Churches can become legalistic and underemphasize grace. They might even deny the resurrection or deity of Jesus. Church leaders may become immoral or unethical. They may even promote loose living in their teaching.

In fact, that's the sort of unfaithfulness that was tempting the Christians at Pergamum. The overt persecution of the Romans did not cause them to crumble at all. Even when Antipas was killed,

---

22 Mark Wilson, *Victory Through The Lamb: A Guide to Revelation in Plain Language*, Wooster, Ohio: Weaver Book Company, 2014, p. 36

they stayed true to the gospel. What got the Pergamum church was corruption from within.

As Warren Wiersbe says,

> Satan had not been able to destroy them by coming as a roaring lion but he was making inroads as a deceiving serpent. [23]

NO CHAMELEONS

In the mockumentary film *Zelig*, Woody Allen plays Leonard Zelig, an enigmatic man who, in his extreme desire to be liked by everyone around him, becomes a human chameleon. He literally takes on the physical characteristics of whomever he is with without even realizing he is changing. The Pergamum Christians were a little like that. They stood firm against outright persecution without any compromise, but were subtly and slowly changing like chameleons to reflect their culture.

In Romans 12:2, the Apostle Paul says, *"Don't become so well-adjusted to your culture that you fit into it without even thinking."* (THE MESSAGE)

In your walk of faith, don't be a Zelig. Live for an audience of one — the one who loves you infinitely, Jesus Christ.

≡ APPLY IT

How does it encourage you to know that Jesus is ultimately the one with the "power of the sword"?

Are you ever tempted to just blend in with the culture? How?

---

23 *The Bible Exposition Commentary: New Testament, Vol. 2.* Victor Publishing, 2001. p. 574

DIGGING DEEPER

The number 7 is used 54 times in the book of Revelation. And it's all over the Bible. From the seven days of Genesis to the seven churches of Revelation, Scripture is saturated with the number seven. It apparently derives its meaning from the creation story: God created the world in six days and rested on the seventh. Most scholars believe that to the original readers, "7" therefore represented completeness and perfection.

In Revelation there are:

- **Seven spirits before God's throne, standing for the infinite perfection of the Holy Spirit** (REV. 1:4)

- **Seven stars in Christ's right hand, demonstrating Jesus' complete authority over the representatives of the churches** (REV. 1:16)

- **Seven horns and seven eyes of the Lamb signifying His perfect power (a horn was a symbol for strength) and complete omniscience (The eye symbolizes the fact that he is all-seeing)** (REV. 5:6)

- **Seven seals written on the scroll, symbolic of the complete plan of history of which Christ is the administrator** (REV. 5:5)

- **Seven trumpets, standing for the completeness of the judgments of God over evil** (REV. 8:2–11:16)

- **Seven bowls, symbolic of the fullness of the wrath of God against evil people** (REV.15:5-8; 16:1–21)

- **Seven rewards of overcomers** (REV. 2 & 3)[24]

In keeping with this interpretation of the number, the seven churches were probably meant to represent the entirety of the various circumstances facing the churches in the 1st century.

---

24 See a more complete discussion in Mike Campagna, "The Number 7 and the Book of Revelation", accessed at http://www.aheartforgod.org/2013/01/11/the-number-7-and-the-book-of-revelation/

17

HOW TO STAY FAITHFUL

"I know where you live—where Satan has his throne. Yet you remain true to my name..." REV. 2:13A NIV

What does it means when Jesus says they live "where Satan has his throne"? There are a lot of scholarly guesses, because there were many religions and cults that might have been seen as Satanic by Jews and Christians of the time.

This phrase could be referring to the cult of Serapis, an Egyptian god who allegedly ruled the underworld and had a huge worship center in Pergamum. He was depicted in statues with a scepter in his hand indicating his rule over the land of the dead, with Cerberus, canine gatekeeper of the underworld, resting at his feet with a snake. During the Flavian dynasty of Roman emperors, the time Revelation was written, Serapis was pictured on Roman coins along with Caesar.

The "seat of Satan" might refer to the Temple of Asclepius, the official god of Pergamum. Sick people would lay on marble floors and allow temple snakes to brush up against them or slither across their bodies, believing these sacred serpents might heal them (Think of that the next time you go to the doctor and that flu shot won't seem so bad!).

The phrase could refer to the massive complex of huge temples on the steep mountainside. From far below these would have looked like a gigantic chair or throne, a "throne of Satan."

This may refer to the fact that Pergamum is the seat, the throne, of Roman authority in the province. There was a temple dedicated to Roma, the goddess of Rome, and to emperor worship here.

I'm not 100% sure, but I think the phrase refers to the unusual collision of all these notorious powers in one place. In any case, it means that the Christians in Pergamum are living in a place that Jesus himself recognizes is unusually full of evil influences and pressures to abandon the faith.

THERE WILL BE A TEST

You and I may never face that kind of combined pressure. No one has ever threatened me with death for my faith. But have no doubt about it: *Your faith will be tested.*

Don't be surprised. Don't be unprepared. It will happen.

At a neighborhood party when you're tempted to water down what you believe.

In the thick of an argument when you're tempted to manipulate a loved one with religious guilt.

In the solitude of an empty house when you're tempted to visit a website you know would be morally compromising.

At work or school when people start making fun of Christians and you feel like slinking off without ever letting anyone know that you're one of those believers yourself.

In a million ways, you and I will find our faithfulness to Jesus tested. The good news in the Book of Revelation is this: You *can* stay faithful!

From the very beginning, Christians just like you have stayed faithful even in the face of death threats.

JESUS GETS IT

And take comfort in this truth. Jesus knows exactly what your cultural situation is like. The phrase *"I know where you live"* might sound a little scary, but that's not how the original readers would have heard it. Jesus is saying, "I know the stress you're under. I know what it's like there. You live in an unusual culture."

But the Christians in Pergamum were not abandoning the faith outright or wilting in the face of Roman death threats. Instead they compromised their faith, little by little, because of teachers within the church family. They knew how to resist outside pressure, but they never expected to deal with twisted doctrine from a very strange teacher on the inside, as we'll see next.

≡ APPLY IT

Do you feel our culture is like Pergamum in some ways? How?

How has your faith been tested recently?

18

WHAT I BELIEVE
CHANGES ME

The Christians in Pergamum were absolutely willing to *die* for Jesus. In fact, some of them already had. But... were they willing to *live* for Jesus? This is where they had a weak spot.

> [Jesus says,] *"There are some among you who hold to the teaching of Balaam, who taught Balak to entice the Israelites to sin so that they ate food sacrificed to idols and committed sexual immorality. Likewise, you also have those who hold to the teaching of the Nicolaitans."* REV. 2:14,15 NIV

Again, here's an obscure reference modern readers need to decode.

You can read all about Balaam and Balak in Numbers 22–25 and 31. Essentially, Balaam was a mysterious sorcerer-for-hire. And Balak, king of Midian, was eager to hire him. It's a story that happens centuries before the events in Revelation 2, when the nation of Israel is journeying through the desert after their Egyptian slavery. Balak wants to destroy the nation of Israel as it pours out of Egypt and through his country. But he knows his army is too weak.

So he hires Balaam, who is some sort of renowned sorcerer, to curse the Israelites. Balaam says, basically, okay, but I can only say what God puts in my mouth. Balak responds, hey, say whatever you want, just make sure you get a good curse in.

Balaam stands up on a hill high above the army of Israel, spreads his arms to prepare the curse, opens his mouth... and out comes a beautiful blessing instead! Balak says, "I told you to curse them! Try again!" Balaam does. Another blessing pours forth. Three times Balaam opens his mouth to curse them, and three times he blesses them instead. Balak is pulling his hair out at this point. It's a funny story!

But Balaam is a slippery character. Later he tells Balak, look, you really don't need to resort to sorcery. It's very simple. Send your prettiest women. Have them dance seductively for the men of Israel. Get the men to fall for them — even to marry them. Because, he says, I guarantee you that once they have those women in their homes, and the women bring out their idols, the Israelite men will begin worshipping idols too. Sexual compromise will lead to ideological and devotional compromise. And that's exactly what happened. That still happens today.

SLOW SLIDE
In our media consumption, our business practices, our thought life, our relationships, our private lives, it is easy to compromise incrementally. Until we are rationalizing away what the Bible clearly says is wrong.

So how does the weird story of Balaam relate to the Christians at Pergamum?

In Pergamum there were several pagan festivals each year when food was offered to the gods and then served up as part of a feast where temple prostitutes would also offer themselves to the revelers. And believers in Pergamum were starting to participate because there were teachers in the church telling them it was okay. They were called the

Nicolaitans. They essentially taught the same thing Balaam did: "It's okay to compromise!"

Here's where it sounds very strange to our modern ears. As we saw earlier, the Nicolaitans apparently taught a form of dualism: Only the *spiritual* is holy; the *physical* world is irredeemably corrupt. So nothing done in the physical world matters, since it's all destined to burn anyway. You can drink to excess or carouse or abuse your body. None of it makes a difference to you spiritually. Or so they taught.

And, since you live in a pagan, immoral culture, why cause problems for yourself? Blend in! Fit in! It won't impact your spiritual life in the least.

Of course this is not a biblical teaching at all. We are physical beings, not just spiritual, and our physical well-being matters to God as much as our spiritual life.

MORE THAN SPIRITS

The Bible teaches that God is intensely concerned with this physical world. That's why Jesus was resurrected physically, and will recreate a new physical earth. You and I are not designed just to be spiritual beings. We are, as C.S. Lewis put it, a kind of amphibian: Both physical and spiritual. And in this life, what we do in one realm impacts the other.

In pointing out the error of the Nicolaitans, Jesus is making an important point. *What you believe matters.* Your theology makes a difference. In fact, it completely changes you.

Many today insist, "It doesn't matter what you believe, as long as you're sincere." But in fact it does matter, very much. How you define reality, how you define the problem with reality, how you define the solution, will change everything about you — your values, your priorities, your commitments, your attitude. And your destiny.

The Christians at Pergamum believed a lie that led them to sin. "The physical world doesn't matter." It was a weird one to modern ears, but we are whispered other lies that lead to the same kind of compromise, lies like: "You deserve it." "God just wants you to be happy." "God wants you to be rich." "You blew it already, so why not go all the way?"

TWO LIES AND A TRUTH

Throughout the history of the Christian church, the lies we believe fall into two camps. You could call one *relativism*, the belief that all moral truth is relative, and so it doesn't matter what you do, as long as you are being true to yourself. The Nicolaitans' error fell into this camp. Relativism leads to immorality and despair.

But Christians have historically overreacted to relativism by veering all the way over into *moralism*. That's the belief that you are saved by your morality, and what you do matters so much that God judges you worthy or unworthy of heaven by your works. That leads to legalism, judgmental attitudes, and also despair.

The way of Christ is a third way, the way of the gospel. As John writes earlier in Revelation:

> To him who loves us and has freed us from our sins by his blood,
> and has made us to be a kingdom and priests to serve his God and
> Father — to him be glory and power for ever and ever! Amen.
>
> REV. 1:5,6 NIV

The gospel of grace recognizes: He loves us. He has freed us. I am saved from sin, not by works, but by the blood of Jesus. He has given me purpose: To serve him as part of his kingdom of priests.

Grace doesn't trivialize sin, but it gives me hope. Only by centering my life on this gospel can I stay true to Jesus, avoiding both relativism on one hand and moralism on the other.

Don't lose your baseline. Stay focused on the gospel. Don't get distracted by some intriguing teaching that encourages you to abandon your core values to get immediate relief from tension.

≡ APPLY IT

Are you more prone to fall into relativism or moralism?

Are there false teachings leading Christians astray today in either direction? Like what?

19

I CAN CHANGE

When Jesus commands the Pergamum church to repent, he is implying an important truth for you and me: *I can change.* There is hope for me. If I fall, I am not doomed.

> *[Jesus says,] "Repent therefore! Otherwise, I will soon come to you and will fight against them with the sword of my mouth."*
>
> REV. 2:16 NIV

This might sound severe, but as Jesus says later, *"Those whom I love I rebuke and discipline"* (REV. 3:19). He is only calling the Pergamum Christians to repentance because he loves them and wants the best for them. And the very fact that he calls them to repentance means there is still hope for them.

"Repent" is a word you might associate with wild-eyed, negative preachers. But the way Jesus uses it, it's not a negative thing. *"Repent"* means God has a better future for you. *"Repent"* means though you may feel lost, you can always turn to Christ. *"Repent"* means God is more interested in people turning back to him than he is in judging them. *"Repent"* is a word of hope and grace. It means all you need to do is turn to him.

THE CORRECTION OF CHRIST

When Jesus says he will fight with "the sword of my mouth" he is referring to the sword of the Spirit, the word of God, not a physical sword. Jesus is going to remove these false teachers from leadership through biblical correction unless they publicly repent and repudiate their false teaching.

This gives me a lot of hope, because sometimes I look at the crazy things being taught in the name of Christ and wonder how so many wacky teachers can gain so many followers. But Jesus is saying here, they won't last long. He'll raise up people who challenge them with the Word, and if they don't receive the correction, they'll be removed from authority. Jesus deeply cares about the leadership of his church.

But he is not just calling the leaders to repentance – he's calling everyone.

As we've seen, repentance, the Greek word *metanoia*, means a change of mind. I change my stinking thinking. I switch my mental direction.

DON'T DELAY

While compromise happens in slow increments, repentance doesn't have to. Take a big positive step mentally. Change the way you see your situation. There's a lot more to recovery than that, but it all begins with an act of repentance, of changing my mind, of accepting what Christ says about the truth of my situation.

Jesus loves you very much, and wants the best for your life. And he loves you enough to call you back onto the right track when you need it.

If you sense right now that he is calling you to repent of something in your life, don't let another day go by without taking action. Pray, "God, I have been allowing my thought life and moral life to be compromised. Help me to change my way of thinking. I want to see the reality of both my sin and the power of your grace. You are my hope, and I trust in your power to save me from this."

Now start thinking of the beauty of Jesus Christ!

≡ APPLY IT

Have you ever despaired that you could ever change?

How is trusting in God's power and not mere will power a key to real change?

20

SPECIAL NAMES AND ENGRAVED INVITATIONS

In an interview on mlb.com, former Dodgers manager Tommy Lasorda talked about the importance of names. He says he knew that pitcher Orel Hershiser, with his weak-looking physique and negative attitude, needed more than just a boost in confidence. A first name like Orel just wasn't going to intimidate fearsome sluggers like Dale Murphy. So Lasorda told him, "I am never going to call you Orel again!" Instead, Lasorda gave him the fearsome nickname: "Bulldog," even though Hershiser had done nothing yet to earn the title. Lasorda says he's convinced that new name made a difference. [25]

Imagine Hershiser facing New York Mets pitcher Ron Darling. From opposing dugouts, Lasorda yells, "Come on, Bulldog!" and Mets manager Davey Johnson yells, "Come on, Darling!" Somehow, as John Ortberg puts it, you just know who's going to win that one.

A NEW NAME
As he closes his letter to the church at Pergamum, Jesus says something that reveals the power of a name:

---

25 Video interview on http://mlb.mlb.com/news/wall/article.jsp?content_id=26106442

> *"Whoever has ears, let them hear what the Spirit says to the*
> *churches. To the one who is victorious, I will give some of the*
> *hidden manna. I will also give that person a white stone with*
> *a new name written on it, known only to the one who receives*
> *it."* REV. 2:17 NIV

Let's decode this. Manna was the bread-like substance that God caused to fall on the ground like dew every day when Moses and the Israelites wandered in the wilderness. In Exodus 16, Moses has a jar of manna placed into the Ark of the Covenant as a reminder for future generations. By the time of Christ, the Ark of the Covenant was long gone from the Temple in Jerusalem.

But where was it? The rabbis disagreed. A late second century Jewish writing known as the *Tosefta* recaps the opinions of several ancient rabbis that, nearly 600 years before Christ, King Josiah of Judah hid the Ark, along with the jar of manna and a jar of holy anointing oil. Supposedly he did this in order to prevent them from being carried off into Babylon. But the legend grew that the hidden manna and the Ark would be revealed when the Messiah came.

Perhaps this is what Jesus is referring to here when he says, *"I will give some of the hidden manna."* What he's saying is, you'll get to eat something far better than anything you can taste at those pagan feasts. Better than anything you could ever imagine. Something you've been waiting for your whole life – because I am the Messiah, and I am coming again. I'm bringing with me the manna that's been hidden for all these years.

But there's more. He says, *"I will also give that person a white stone with a new name written on it, known only to the one who receives it."*

When I was in Pergamum, I looked down and noticed the ground was covered with little flat white stones. They seem to exist in abundance in this area. I'll admit here that I slipped one of those stones into my pocket.

The Romans had several uses for these stones, which they called *tesserae*. Because they are flat and white they were perfect for engraving or writing on.

An athlete who won his or her event was given tesserae that entitled the holder to eat for free at public feasts.

The Roman elite used tesserae as invitations to parties or banquets.

Panels of judges would write their verdict on tesserae if the defendant was found innocent.

Clearly for Pergamum society, the white stone had many layers of meaning, which all had spiritual parallels. The tesserae could be seen as an award, an invitation, an acquittal.

But here's my favorite use of these white stones:.

Friends made special pacts with them: You'd take the flat stone and cut it in two. Your friend's half would have a nickname chosen for you by your friend, and you'd have your friend's name. And from then on, you'd always be welcome in each other's homes. Even after your death, if one of your descendants presented the stone at one of your friend's descendants' homes, they would be welcomed in. All because of the special name written on the stone. Because you would choose a nickname known only to close intimates and family. That name was hidden. Secret. Like a password.

I believe this verse is saying that one day you will stand before the God who made you, and he will hand you an engraved invitation that means you will always be welcome at his feast. And on it will be Jesus' secret nickname for you. I think it will be the word you've most wanted to hear your whole life. Something God sees in you, and has created in you. *Courageous. Beautiful. Beloved. Faithful.*

When heaven and earth are recreated, and you are resurrected, you and I tend to think of how beautiful everything around us will be. But you and I will be a part of the beauty too. Like the earth itself, like all the saints, you will be, as C.S. Lewis put it, "a creature of unimaginable splendor." And God will see that and put a name on it.

For that, it's worth staying faithful.

≡ **APPLY IT**

How does this vision of the rewards that await help motivate you to stay faithful to Jesus?

21

HOPE FOR THE COMPROMISERS

Let's recap what we've learned in Pergamum. Jesus says to this church, basically, "I know you're in a very weird, difficult place where you are being pressured to deny my name. I know you are refusing to do that, even in the face of death. But you have a weak spot. You won't technically deny me, but you are embracing a theology that will allow you to morally compromise, and ultimately that is going to weaken the church just as much as persecution. Because the distinction between you and everyone else will erode until there's no difference."

And this is important for you and me to hear. If life is hard, we're struggling, we're suffering, we can start to imagine we have permission to indulge our sinful tendencies a little bit.

And Jesus says, "No." He says, "I acknowledge, I understand, the complex situation you are ministering in. Nevertheless, it doesn't excuse sin."

Three points to remember, paraphrased from my good friend Curt Harlow:

1. Choose whether you'll be shaped at your deepest level of thinking by your culture or by Christ.

American Christianity has followed in the footsteps of the Pergamum church in many ways. We invite, convert, and baptize new believers. Then they all spend their lives living exactly like the rest of the world. There is a deep level where the gospel of truth needs to be changing us on the inside, and bubbling up into our moral choices.

2. Theology leads to action.

What you believe matters. Who you listen to matters. How you think matters. It all leads to action, good or bad.

3. One of God's greatest gifts is the invitation to repent.

God is waiting to help you. But you and I need to change our thinking, acknowledge where we are messed up, and turn our lives over to him.

≡ APPLY IT

How have you seen God help you in your life when you have repented — that is, changed your thinking?

Some of the few remains of ancient Thyatira in the small archaeological park in the center of the modern city
Photo credit: www.HolyLandPhotos.org

THE FOURTH LETTER

22

TO CHRISTIANS IN A CULTURE OF TOLERANCE

We've talked a lot so far about the ruins of ancient churches. But here's the story of much newer ruins: The remains of a place in the Santa Cruz Mountains, near my home, called "Holy City".

If you drive there today you'll see a few abandoned buildings. There's hardly a trace of what was once a bizarre religious cult, and one of the weirdest tourist attractions in the Bay Area.

Holy City offered travellers barbecue, dancing, drinking, movies... and messages from God. In 1919, a man calling himself Father Riker claimed to receive "messages from God through my nerves" (people get on my nerves; does that count?). He started Holy City, calling it "heaven on earth." His congregation there was the "Perfect Christian Divine Way Church."

Three hundred disciples lived in the commune. All money went to Riker. There were no marriages allowed. Except for Riker, of course, who had four wives at the same time.

Riker was a racist who said God told him only whites should rule the world. His personal church thugs were suspected of beating and kidnapping defectors from the movement. He broadcast increasingly bizarre messages from his radio station there until faced with legal problems. He sold Holy City in 1957. Arsonists burned most of it, and he died in a hospital in 1969 at the age of 96 — but not before he converted to Christianity and recanted many of his previous views.

I wish I could say Holy City was an exception.

THE DECLINE OF PEOPLE'S TEMPLE

Remember People's Temple? It was a well-known church in San Francisco pastored by Rev. Jim Jones. People's Temple won civic awards. Politicians like Walter Mondale, Jerry Brown, Willie Brown, and George Moscone all applauded its good works. It was a member in good standing of the "Disciples of Christ" denomination. At its height it counted an incredible 20,000 members.

But then things got weird. Jim Jones started justifying his sexual promiscuity of all kinds. He taught that only he, God's sole living prophet, knew the real message of Jesus. A thousand members moved to the jungles of Guyana to start a utopia. His acolytes murdered United States representatives who came to investigate. Then on November 18, 1978, 900 of them died there when their leaders told them to drink punch that had been deliberately poisoned.

Just like Holy City, the buildings of People's Temple have vanished. In Guyana, the jungle has swallowed them up. And in October 1989, the Loma Prieta earthquake damaged the People's Temple building on Geary Street so badly that it had to be completely bulldozed. Basically no trace of the church remains.

Or does it?

The Bible says that what happened at Holy City or People's Temple can happen at any church. Good people believed false teachers who eventually led them to horribly immoral behavior and destruction.

KILLING A CULT

Jesus speaks to a church facing this exact problem in his letter to Thyatira. This is the longest of the seven letters, even though it's written to the smallest church, facing the least persecution. It is in some ways the most complex of the seven letters. Ready? Here we go:

> "Write this letter to the angel of the church in Thyatira. This is the message from the Son of God, whose eyes are like flames of fire, whose feet are like polished bronze:
>
> "I know all the things you do. I have seen your love, your faith, your service, and your patient endurance. And I can see your constant improvement in all these things.
>
> "But I have this complaint against you. You are permitting that woman — that Jezebel who calls herself a prophet — to lead my servants astray. She teaches them to commit sexual sin and to eat food offered to idols. I gave her time to repent, but she does not want to turn away from her immorality.
>
> "Therefore, I will throw her on a bed of suffering, and those who commit adultery with her will suffer greatly unless they repent and turn away from her evil deeds. I will strike her children dead. Then all the churches will know that I am the one who searches out the thoughts and intentions of every person. And I will give to each of you whatever you deserve.
>
> "But I also have a message for the rest of you in Thyatira who have not followed this false teaching ('deeper truths,' as they call them — depths of Satan, actually). I will ask nothing more of you except that you hold tightly to what you have until I come. To all who are victorious, who obey me to the very end, to them I will give authority over all the nations.
>
> "They will rule the nations with an iron rod and smash them like clay pots.

They will have the same authority I received from my Father, and I will also give them the morning star!

"Anyone with ears to hear must listen to the Spirit and understand what he is saying to the churches." REV. 2:18-29 NLT

There are a lot of things here that may trouble you, so please remember this is written in the style of apocalyptic literature – it's largely symbolic, not literal. So what do all these references mean? We'll explore it all, but first remember the big picture:

Tolerance is a very high virtue in our Western culture. And we sometimes forget there's a difference between tolerating someone's right to *teach* anything they want in the broader society and our responsibility to be discerning about what we *believe* as Christians. Tolerance does not mean unthinking acceptance of everyone's viewpoint. Because there are some ideas that can lead to a lot of pain. Particularly religious ideas.

C. S. Lewis famously said, "Of all bad men, religious bad men are the worst." [26] Church history – and today's headlines – reveal his words to be true.

What you believe about God, how to be directed by Him, and how to please Him will profoundly impact your life and the lives of everyone around you.

≡ APPLY IT

Why is it so important to be careful about what you believe?

Do you tend to be discerning or gullible?

---

26 C.S. Lewis, *Reflections on the Psalms*. Boston: Houghton, Mifflin, Harcourt, 1964. p. 32

23

FEET OF CLAY OR
FEET OF BRONZE

Today, Thyatira is known as the bustling Turkish city of Akhisar. There's not much to see here. The archaeological remains of ancient Thyatira are located within a single fenced off city block right in the heart of Akhisar.

Archaeologists have found no trace of a theater or stadium or any of the other entertainment diversions that existed in the other cities of Revelation. Only shops and traces of one temple. And more inscriptions naming more trade guilds than in any other ancient site yet discovered. Apparently, in Thyatira, the people were all business.

Thyatira was about 35 miles southeast of Pergamum. In New Testament times it was a small city, but a very busy one. The city stood at the junction of three main roads leading to Pergamum, Sardis, and Smyrna. And because of that, a lot of merchants settled here. It was a fantastic location for business because of the triple junction of these trade routes.

Intriguingly, there is no record of any Roman persecution of Christians in Thyatira, or any sense that there was tension here in the synagogue between the Jews and Christians. And yet these Christians, facing no religious persecution, ended up being the ones in greatest danger, and merited the longest and most intense correction from Jesus.

Here's why. The merchants of the town built a colossal main street that went right through the center of town, lined with large shops and the city's trade guilds. Everyone who worked in the city had to be a member of one or more of these guilds, which functioned somewhat like workers' unions today, but with even more power. It was very tough to make a living in Thyatira without belonging to one of these societies.

Each trade guild had its own patron deity, sort of like a "sponsor god." We know from history that the meetings of the guilds were regularly devoted to orgies connected to the worship of erotic idols. So to attend the "union meetings" was to become involved with the worship of idols, gluttony, and sexual immorality. Christians were rightly disturbed at this kind of revelry, but in order to work in Thyatira you had to be in one of these guilds. What was a Christian to do?

Jesus begins his letter with an intriguing description of himself:

> "This is the message from the Son of God, whose eyes are like flames of fire, whose feet are like polished bronze." REV. 2:18 NLT

Let's do some decoding.

THE TRUE SON OF GOD

In Thyatira there was a Temple of Apollo, who was referred to as "the Son of God" in Greek literature. There was also a huge bronze industry, where the people would have seen refining fires burning every day.

Keep that in mind as we look for more clues in that other ancient apocalyptic book of prophecies, the Book of Daniel. In chapter 10, Daniel has a vision of a being from heaven:

I looked up and saw a man dressed in linen clothing, with a belt of pure gold around his waist. His body looked like a precious gem. His face flashed like lightning, and his eyes flamed like torches. His arms and feet shone like polished bronze, and his voice roared like a vast multitude of people. DANIEL 10:5,6 NLT

Sound familiar? In Revelation 2, Jesus is combining imagery the Thyatirans would recognize from their own culture with these images from the Jewish Scriptures to say:

I am the Son of God. The living Jesus, not a statue of Apollo, or any other alleged Son of God, is the one we are to heed and respect.

My eyes are like fire. Just like the image in Daniel. This means, in modern terms, Jesus' eyes are like a divine laser. They can see your problems before you can see them. They can see issues you are trying to hide from everyone else. And they can refine you like metal refined in a furnace.

My feet are like polished bronze. In Daniel, this image is meant to be a contrast with an earlier vision. In Daniel 2, there is a vision of a human kingdom that appears glorious. It looks like a man with a head of gold and chest of silver and thighs of bronze. Seems very substantial and impressive, except for one important detail. The statue has feet of iron mixed with clay (See Daniel 2:31-45). As beautiful as the golden top of the statue is, its clay feet are unstable and easily smashed. That's meant to represent the beauty — and instability — of a human empire.

Then in Daniel 10, he sees a man from heaven, not earth — *and he has feet not of clay, but of bronze.* This means that God's kingdom cannot be smashed like human kingdoms with their superficial beauty but feet of clay.

That's the point of this imagery in Revelation, too. Jesus is telling the Thyatiran Christians that the glories of Rome, including the great businesses and wide streets of their city, may seem built to last, but they won't. So don't devote your whole life to them. *Don't give first class allegiance to second class causes.* Only the kingdom of God will last.

Like the Thyatirans, we can be faced with temptations to compromise at work and in our broader culture. But human beings and all they build are like that statue with a head of gold and feet of clay.

You and I face decisions every day about how to spend our time, how to set priorities, who to pay attention to. At the very foundation of your decision making should be this: Is the thing to which I am devoting my time and money and energy going to last? In other words, does it have feet of bronze or feet of clay?

≡ APPLY IT

What parts of our culture would you say are like the statue with a head of gold, but feet of clay?

Ask God to help you make decisions based on what will last forever.

DIGGING DEEPER

How do I handle the troubling parts of Revelation?

If the parts of the Bible with troubling prophesies about the turbulent future like the Book of Revelation ever make you feel uneasy, then you are not alone.

In the apocalyptic sections of Book of Daniel, a messenger from heaven shows Daniel a vision of the future very similar to parts of Revelation, and Daniel is upset. He writes, *"My strength left me, my face grew deathly pale, and I felt very weak."* (DANIEL 10:8)

But God comforts him:

> *"Just then a hand touched me and lifted me, still trembling, to my hands and knees. And the man said to me, 'Daniel, you are very precious to God, so listen carefully to what I have to say to you. Stand up, for I have been sent to you.' When he said this to me, I stood up, still trembling. Then he said, 'Don't be afraid, Daniel.'"* DANIEL 10:10,11

After more of the vision, Daniel writes this:

> *"I said to the one standing in front of me, 'I am filled with anguish because of the vision I have seen, my lord, and I am very weak...' Then the one who looked like a man touched me again, and I felt my strength returning. 'Don't be afraid,' he said, 'for you are very precious to God. Peace! Be encouraged! Be strong!'"* DANIEL 10:16,18

This is a great template for how to respond to the Book of Revelation. Its visions can trouble us, and that's okay, because some *are* troubling. But ultimately, the message they are meant to convey to believers is one of hope. They are in the Bible precisely because, like Daniel, you are very precious to God. And he wants you to be encouraged. Be strong because you know who will last, and who will win the victory in the end.

24

DON'T ASSUME
YOU'RE IMMUNE

Remember, the letter to Thyatira was written because the church had been tolerating unbiblical teaching. Basically it was turning into a cult. How does this happen?

We live in a society that values everyone's right to teach and believe whatever they want. Even in churches, it seems intolerant, and maybe even a little impolite and rebellious, to say, "This leader is teaching something unbiblical." But that attitude allows insidious error to creep in that turns a healthy church into something like the People's Temple.

So how do you know when you've crossed the line from healthy tolerance and respect to unhealthy gullibility?

There are four ways to stay discerning about teachers in these verses. Let's examine them this week.

First: *Don't assume you're immune.*

If you hear stories like the ones I told earlier in these pages about the Holy City and People's Temple and think, *Bro-ther! I would never fall for that*, consider this:

A play called "The People's Temple" opened ten years ago at the Berkeley Repertory Theater, based on dozens of interviews with surviving church members including Jim Jones' own son.

The point of the play? These were normal people. As one former member put it at the premiere of the play, "We were grandmothers, sisters, just regular folks." They were smart. The assistant district attorney of San Francisco was one of the elders. They were effective. Their addiction treatment center weaned 300 addicts off drugs. They were involved. Their food pantry fed more people than any other church in San Francisco.

But they slowly accepted more and more weirdness in their church leadership. And Jesus is saying, what happened to them can happen to you and me if we do not stay alert.

> "I know all the things you do. I have seen your love, your faith, your service, and your patient endurance. And I can see your constant improvement in all these things." REV. 2:19 NLT

Jesus names six positives. They were loving, unlike the Ephesians. They had strong faith. They served others. They endured for Jesus. They did not cave. They were improving, their church was apparently growing. These people looked like model citizens. And we *should* do these things. These are not wrong.

That's important, because occasionally I hear critics say that a church emphasizing service to the poor is bound to become liberal theologically. But service is important. That's not what's being criticized here; it's being commended. Jesus fed the hungry, healed the sick, welcomed the children and women and other marginalized parts of his society. And the lifestyle of Christ-followers should reflect the lifestyle of Christ.

But in the midst of all this great activity, the Thyatirans dropped their guard in one crucial area.

"But I have this complaint against you. You are permitting that woman — that Jezebel who calls herself a prophet — to lead my servants astray." REV. 2:20A NLT

The only problem in this church — and it was a fatal error — was allowing someone to teach falsehood. How did they let their guard down in this area? Perhaps they themselves could see all the good in their church. Then as they began to think about how loving they were, how faithful they were, how much they were improving, they began to let down their guard just a little bit.

FINDING JEZEBEL

Let's do some more decoding.

In Thyatira a woman of prominence in the church was turning into what we would call a cult leader.

Jesus calls this woman "Jezebel." That was not her actual name. No one in those days would have named a baby girl Jezebel. It would be like naming a boy "Hitler" today. In the Old Testament, centuries before the Book of Revelation was written, Jezebel was the wife of King Ahab of Israel. She is infamous for making the worship of the god Baal popular in Israel.

Baal was a fertility god, and his worship involved sexual immorality. Often in ancient times people practiced "sympathetic magic," which meant that you rehearsed in the miniaturized world of the pagan temples a small version of what you were praying would happen in the larger world, in your country, or in your family. For example, if you prayed for family fertility or farm productivity, you'd go to a temple and participate in temple prostitution. Acts of fertility. It's like you were helping the gods understand what it was you were asking for.

Not a good idea. This spiraled all the way into human sacrifice, for reasons still unclear. Perhaps the idea was that if we killed one of our enemies at the temple, the gods would kill more.

And it was all popularized by Jezebel.

Now hundreds of years later, that name is being used to describe this false teacher in Thyatiran Christian circles.

I want to make it clear that it was not her *gender* that Jesus is criticizing here. It was her *teaching*. There were other female leaders in the Old Testament, like Deborah, who were great. In the New Testament, Philip had four daughters who were all prophets. It's interesting to me that the first person we meet in the Bible from Thyatira is a woman named Lydia, a dealer in purple cloth who becomes a follower of Jesus in Acts 16 after hearing Paul while she's on a business trip to Philippi. The trouble with Jezebel is not that she's a *female* prophet. It's that she's a *false* prophet.

And this great church is falling for it.

Good, helpful, loving, faithful people can be led astray by false teaching. The best, most loving and faithful people can be fooled by some Pied Piper.

And they weren't the only ones. The Apostle Paul said to the Galatians,

> *I am astonished that you are so quickly deserting the one who called you to live in the grace of Christ and are turning to a different gospel — which is really no gospel at all. Evidently some people are throwing you into confusion and are trying to pervert the gospel of Christ.* GALATIANS 1:6,7 NIV

He pointed out to the Corinthians,

> *If someone comes to you and preaches a Jesus other than the Jesus we preached... or a different gospel from the one you accepted, you put up with it easily enough.* 2 CORINTHIANS 11:4 NIV

So how do you stay on guard? We will find out next.

≡ APPLY IT

Why would anyone assume they were immune to the lure of false teaching? Why are Christians gullible at times?

What do you think is the best way to stay on guard and yet not get so cynical that you just stop getting involved with church and with Christian service?

25

INSTALL YOUR THEOLOGICAL SPAM FILTER

I found a pamphlet written by Jim Jones where he says, "We must have a living prophet to direct us. I have come to make God real. I am causing untold thousands to believe in Jesus by the great miracles I perform! Oh, what a privilege it is to personify the mind of God."

Sadly, Christian history is filled with teachers who claim this kind of divine authority. Far from being just quaint or weird, they're dangerous.

Think about it. Jesus says next to nothing about corrupt politicians or corrupt entertainers or anyone else in the broader society. But he consistently criticizes corrupt religious leaders.

And he does so here too. Jesus asks the Thyatiran church, "Why do you tolerate this fake prophet?"

> *"By her teaching she misleads my servants into sexual immorality and the eating of food sacrificed to idols."* REV. 2:20 NIV

What was her teaching?

WHAT HAPPENS IN THYATIRA STAYS IN THYATIRA

Remember, in this city, in order to work, Christians had to join a pagan trade guild. Some of the guild meetings each year would be devoted to orgies that involved both gluttonous eating of food that had been part of a pagan ritual, and sexual immorality with temple prostitutes.

And apparently "Jezebel" is teaching, "It's okay, you need to make a living. God understands. He'll overlook this. Business is business." Kind of an ancient version of, "What happens in Vegas, stays in Vegas."

Let's make this very personal. Just as for the church at Thyatira, for most of us, our enemies are not emperors in amphitheaters. It's your nine to five occupation. Wherever you work is the place of greatest temptation to compromise.

These Christians did not have big stadiums where they were commanded to deny Christ before the crowds or get burned at the stake. They just had little private altars in the secret ceremonies of their trade guilds. But you know what? For most of us, that kind of pressure is harder to resist than the big-time stadium pressure. And this false teacher is whispering, "Go ahead."

HOW TO SPOT FALSE TEACHERS

So how can I spot false teachers? In Jesus' warning to these Christians there are *three common signs of false teachers:*

• **A love of authority and titles.**

He describes Jezebel as someone who, *"calls herself a prophet."* Calling *herself* a prophet. Not waiting for the church at large to confirm this gift, but saying, "Hey, I am a special voice of God! I have God's private line."

• **Refusal to take correction.**

Why? Because of that alleged connection to God! Jesus says, *"I have given her time to repent, but she is unwilling."* (REV. 2:21 NIV)

• **Claims of secret teaching not found in Scripture**

You might want to highlight that phrase, underline it, star it, memorize it. Why? This is one thing that so many false teachers have in common, but that seems to lure followers every time.

Jesus describes, *"Satan's so-called deep secrets"* (REV. 2:24B NIV) or *"deeper truths,' as they call them — depths of Satan, actually."* (REV. 2:24B NLT)

People love the word "secret." It appeals to our human longing for mystery. It seems any TV show or book that has "secret" in the title is an instant bestseller. As I write, Amazon has 36,180 books with the word "secrets" in the title. We love it. Even in Christian bookstores. Hidden gospels. Lost teachings. Secret truths. We can't get enough! That's why, even in this study, I've tried to emphasize that decoding the symbolism is a matter of understanding the historical situation of the first readers, not of receiving extra mystical revelation that explains these verses.

I've noticed over the years that many Christians seem to be on a constant hunt for something new. Something different. The next revelation. Usually they say things that make this search seem mature instead of superficial, things like, "I'm looking for something deeper." But often a feeling of superiority begins to creep in if they feel they have insider information, insights others don't have. This is where cultic movements will hook even long-time believers.

It's the age-old error someone has called "Christ Plus." Beware of churches that seem to regularly emphasize Christ Plus. Christ plus extra secrets. Christ plus new prophecies. Christ plus new rules and techniques. Christ plus the leader's opinions on everything from politics to fashion.

Really, the key to the Christian life is to keep it simply focused on Christ *alone*. There's not much more to it than, *"Love the Lord your God with all your heart, soul, mind, and strength, and love your neighbor as yourself."* Everything else is connected to and hinges on that great commandment. But the biggest mistake many believers make is revealed by Jesus in his next words to the Thyatirans.

≡ APPLY IT

Why do you think false teachers like Jezebel or Jim Jones always seem to find followers?

Why is it that even long-term believers can be led astray by false teaching? What is its appeal to them?

26

DON'T CONFUSE SUCCESS WITH BLESSING

One of the main ways false teachers lure so many into their movements is their façade of success. They seem rich, happy, good-looking, and healthy.

But Jesus reminds the church at Thyatira not to confuse success with blessing.

In America we tend to think, if someone's powerful or prosperous, well, how can you argue with success? They must be doing something right! But I once read a statement I've never forgotten: *Prosperity may show God's patience, not God's approval.*

That's what Jesus is saying here:

> *"I gave her time to repent, but she does not want to turn away from her immorality. Therefore, I will throw her on a bed of suffering, and those who commit adultery with her will suffer greatly unless they repent and turn away from her evil deeds."* REV. 2:21,22 NLT

Jesus says, "*I have given her time...*" But sadly, as *The Message* translation of this verse puts it, "*She has no intention of giving up her career in the God business.*"

Maybe you sometimes wish God would judge other people instantly. But he loves them. He's patient. Maybe you feel like they're getting away with something. But God knows. He's just giving them time to repent.

And he's giving *you* time. Perhaps you feel like, "After so long, God must not want me back." Remember the story of the Prodigal Son? When he finally returns home, the father runs to him, kisses him, puts a beautiful robe and ring on him, and throws him a feast! That's how God welcomes *you* home. So if you've been away, come home today.

Jesus is not like a codependent family member who constantly enables your self-destructive behavior. At some point after giving warnings he will let you hit bottom — if that is the only way he might convince you that change is needed.

THERE ARE CONSEQUENCES

I don't know whether he is literally saying this "Jezebel" will end up in a bed of suffering, like a hospital bed, or whether this is a symbolic way of saying that her bed of sexual pleasure will turn into a bed of sorrow and pain.

What about when he later says, *"I will strike her children dead"*? It's a troubling verse. But I do not believe he is literally saying he will kill infants, an image at total odds with the Jesus of the gospels who welcomes little children. Remember this is symbolic language. I believe he is referring to her *ideological* children, her disciples and their little groups. He is saying that he will remove them from their places of influence in the church; he will kill their *movement*.

The point in these verses is simply what we have all discovered in our own lives. There are always consequences to sin.

Whether psychological consequences, health consequences, relational consequences, emotional consequences, career consequences — there will be some sort of reaction to every action.

Sometimes in his grace God keeps us from some consequences we deserve. But sometimes God lets us go through pain in order to reach us and hopefully change us. It's tough love.

God is patient. But don't mistake his patience for approval. One day, out of love, he may decide to let you hit bottom if you don't respond to his patient calls to return home.

≡ APPLY IT

How has God been patient with you, and prevented you from living out the consequences you might have experienced from your sin? Thank him for his mercy.

Have you ever seen God, in his mercy, let you experience consequences so that you hit bottom and come to your senses? It might be difficult to do, but can you in faith thank him for his goodness to you, even in letting you hit bottom?

27

DON'T COMPLICATE
YOUR FAITH

Remember, all false teaching amounts to *Christ Plus*.

Even the false teaching you tell yourself.

If you're thinking, *I'd never lower my guard against the likes of Father Riker or Jim Jones*, hold on. Most of the time the false teacher in your life — is you.

Jesus says,

> "But I also have a message for the rest of you in Thyatira who have not followed this false teaching ('deeper truths,' as they call them — depths of Satan, actually). I will ask nothing more of you except that you hold tightly to what you have until I come."
> REV. 2:24,25 NLT

Such a contrast to the false teachers! No more so-called deep truths. Just hold on tightly to what you already have.

This is a theme throughout the New Testament. You and I don't need "deeper teaching." We need to go deeper into what we *already have* — the gospel.

You see this warning against Christ-plus teaching, and admonishment to have a simple devotion to Christ alone, again and again in Paul's writings. Remember, he is opposing *religion* that complicates Christianity.

> But I fear that somehow your pure and simple devotion to Christ will be corrupted, just as Eve was deceived by the cunning ways of the serpent. 2 CORINTHIANS 11:3 NLT

> Now that you know God (or should I say, now that God knows you), why do you want to go back again and become slaves once more to the weak and useless spiritual principles of this world? GALATIANS 4:9 NLT

> After starting your new lives in the Spirit, why are you now trying to become perfect by your own human effort? GALATIANS 3:3B NLT

> You must continue to believe this truth and stand firmly in it. Don't drift away from the assurance you received when you heard the Good News. COLOSSIANS 1:23 NLT

> Just as you accepted Christ Jesus as your Lord, you must continue to follow him. Let your roots grow down into him, and let your lives be built on him. COLOSSIANS 2:6,7 NLT

> Don't let anyone capture you with empty philosophies and high-sounding nonsense that come from human thinking and from the spiritual powers of this world, rather than from Christ. COL. 2:8 NLT

The next time someone tells you they have a new teaching, a new prophesy, a new angle, a new emphasis, pray that you will see it with discernment, and ask, "Is this part of a pure and simple devotion to Jesus, or is this a slightly different gospel that depends on human effort instead of God's power?"

I'm not speaking here of necessary and productive grappling with the deep truths of the Bible. That's not complicating your faith; it's plunging deeper into gospel basics. I'm talking about the constant hunger for novelty, for the latest new teaching.

Instead, hold tightly to what you already have!

☰ APPLY IT

How can Christians complicate their faith? Have you ever done this? In what ways?

Today, spend some time simply focusing on the love of Christ for you expressed in the gospel of grace. Ask God to help you renew your pure and simple devotion to Christ.

28

TRUTH AND LOVE

Jesus concludes his letter to the Thyatiran church,

"To all who are victorious, who obey me to the very end, to them I will give authority over all the nations. They will rule the nations with an iron rod and smash them like clay pots. They will have the same authority I received from my Father, and I will also give them the morning star! Anyone with ears to hear must listen to the Spirit and understand what he is saying to the churches." REV. 2:26-29

These marginalized Christians, in a world where the Roman government of Domitian looks like it's made of gold and silver and bronze, are told it will all be broken like clay pots. And it was.

Of course Jesus is not advocating violence. He is saying that those now marginalized will one day have authority. The last shall be made first. The lowest shall be exalted.

In those days the goddess Venus was called "the morning star." Here again Jesus takes an image associated with a pagan deity and reclaims it. He is saying that neither Venus nor any other so-called gods are the bright and morning star. He is. And he will give the faithful ones direction like a guiding star, as we stay focused on him.

So the big picture in Thyatira is this: These people are good on all fronts, except they are not discerning enough about a so-called "prophet" in their church. And this is a fatal flaw unless corrected immediately. They need to develop wisdom in this area.

THE BALANCING ACT

And that leads to this question: Where's the balance between being too tolerant on one hand, and too judgmental on the other?

These verses we've been studying are not criticizing the Christians for living in a city where there is immorality and idol worship. They are not being judged for having pagans as friends or as business clients. Jesus is not calling Christians to burn down the Greek temples and the trade guild altars. Christianity was never meant to be a faith of violence or coercion, as any reading of the gospels will tell you. In fact, we are specifically told to live at peace with our neighbors and to communicate our reasons for faith with gentleness and respect (1 Peter 3:15,16). We *propose*, we do not *impose*.

But *within the church* it is right to be concerned about teaching and morality.

There are three possible approaches to error within the church:

TRUTH MINUS LOVE = LEGALISM

This is the error of the Pharisees. They carried around a spiritual measuring tape to see who measured up — but they didn't love them.

You might have grown up in a church with an angry preacher and an angry congregation. The only memories you have of church are rules upon rules. It seemed like every church but your own was harshly criticized for some failing. But there was little love. That's legalism.

LOVE MINUS TRUTH = LICENSE

This is the error of the "Jezebel" in Thyatira. Anything goes. Nothing is a sin. "How can it be wrong? God understands. He is love, after all." Someone once said we can be so open-minded that our brains fall out.

We start with small rationalizations, but soon we stretch the boundaries of acceptable behavior further and further. And soon we're rationalizing behavior we *never* thought we'd participate in.

Those are both extremes. So what's the balance?

TRUTH PLUS LOVE = A CHRIST-LIKE ATTITUDE

Be discerning but not unbiblically strict. Be loving but not overindulgent.

How do I do this in a practical way? Remember, even the Apostle Paul had to admit there were some issues of behavior that God-honoring Christians will simply disagree about. He writes one whole chapter of the Bible, Romans 14, all about this.

Here are a few questions to ask to help you stay discerning about any issue:

1. How does this relate to the core teachings of the Bible?

Is this a major or a minor issue? Your standard is not culture. It is Scripture. But even within the Bible, some issues are apparently minor. Or not even mentioned at all.

As one ancient Christian said, *"In the essentials, unity. In the non-essentials, diversity. In all things, charity (or love)."*

2. What would my spiritual role models advise?

Who do you hold in high esteem? What would Billy Graham or Mother Teresa or the early church fathers be likely to say about this?

3. Is this a compromise for me personally, or am I judging others for their own decisions?

The churches in Revelation 2 and 3 are not being called to account for things that others in their cities did or thought. They are being called to account for their own compromises. And their compromises are not minor issues. They are personally committing sin or accepting false doctrine.

4. Does this distract from a pure and simple devotion to Christ?

Am I simply focused on Christ, or am I adding to that? Is this reflecting and increasing my love for the Lord? This focus is the strong foundation that will be your protection against false teaching.

≡ **APPLY IT**

Ask God to help you develop a discerning spirit that is not a critical spirit.

The Roman-era gymnasium at Sardis

THE FIFTH LETTER

29

TO PEOPLE WHOSE FAITH IS DYING

When I visited Turkey the ruins at Sardis were among the first I saw during my trip, and it was a great way to start. The stunning gymnasium and beautiful synagogue are largely intact, revealing the immense scale and spectacular craftsmanship of the ancient Greco-Roman world.

A hundred yards away from the gymnasium, down an unpaved road, I walked into the remains of the massive Temple of Artemis. Its location in a glen filled with vibrant wildflowers, elegant trees, murmuring streams, and steep hills makes these ruins wildly romantic. This is the Greek world of everyone's imagination. You almost expect to catch a satyr or faun peeking around the collapsed columns of the ancient temple.

But the most famous ruins of Sardis are on the top of the hill just behind the temple. That's where the city fortress loomed, a dizzying 1,500 feet above the valley floor. You can still see crumbling walls on a promontory that juts out from a long mountain range. On three sides, steeply eroded cliffs plunge vertically to the valley. On the fourth side, where it connects to the mountain range, the path is very narrow and drops off precipitously on either edge. It's easy to see why a fortress built up here was long considered absolutely impregnable. Yet two of the most unusual defeats in the history of warfare took place right on this spot.

Five centuries before Christ, the last independent king to rule here, Croesus, went to the Oracle of Delphi to ask if he should go to war against King Cyrus of Persia. The oracle told him that if he did, "a great empire would be destroyed." Based on that prophecy, he attacked Cyrus — but was badly beaten and forced to retreat home to Sardis.

Cyrus gave chase and found Croesus in this fortress high on a hill, surrounded by walls and cliffs, seemingly unreachable. Cyrus offered a reward to any of his soldiers who could discover a way to enter the city. One soldier noticed a defender climbing down a hidden goat trail to recover a helmet he had dropped from above. The Persian soldier memorized the route, scaled the cliffs with some troops, and was shocked to find the city completely unguarded.

Apparently Croesus' soldiers had been so confident that the city's defenses were unbreachable that they had failed to keep watch. And like thieves in the night, the Persians slipped in unnoticed. History records the shock of the defeat as people woke up in the fortress to find enemy soldiers in control and their king taken prisoner.

It seems the oracle of Delphi hedged her bets: The "destroyed kingdom" was that of Croesus, not Cyrus.

A similar event occurred almost 200 years later when the Syrian warrior Antiochus attacked and conquered the still overconfident city. He and a small band of elite troops went up a little path at night, scaled the walls, and again found the city asleep, unguarded, with a reputation for strength — but as good as dead.

Jesus makes the same critique of the church here in his letter to the Christian community at Sardis.

"Write this letter to the angel of the church in Sardis. This is the message from the one who has the sevenfold Spirit of God and the seven stars:

"I know all the things you do, and that you have a reputation for being alive — but you are dead. Wake up! Strengthen what little remains, for even what is left is almost dead. I find that your actions do not meet the requirements of my God.

"Go back to what you heard and believed at first; hold to it firmly. Repent and turn to me again. If you don't wake up, I will come to you suddenly, as unexpected as a thief.

"Yet there are some in the church in Sardis who have not soiled their clothes with evil. They will walk with me in white, for they are worthy. All who are victorious will be clothed in white. I will never erase their names from the Book of Life, but I will announce before my Father and his angels that they are mine.

"Anyone with ears to hear must listen to the Spirit and understand what he is saying to the churches." REV. 3:1-6 NLT

See how he's referring to the history of the city? The Christians here would have known that story well. Croesus was a tragic example of false reputation, self-deception, and lazy unpreparedness. But Jesus is saying, you are repeating your own history!

STAY AWAKE AND STAY ALERT

He's saying, don't drop your guard like your city did. You see yourself as a strong fortress. But the fact is, you're asleep. Weak. Vulnerable. So Jesus tells these believers, "Wake up!" He himself is coming one day "like a thief," he says, as unexpectedly as those Persian soldiers. Don't be caught sleeping when Christ returns.

DECODING THE SYMBOLS

What are we to make of the way Jesus identifies himself at the beginning of this letter? The "sevenfold spirit" probably is meant to indicate that the Spirit of God is perfect, since the number seven in apocalyptic literature is often used symbolically to indicate completion or perfection.

And the seven stars? They represent the seven angels or messengers to the churches as we saw in Revelation 1:20, but they also had another meaning to anyone who ever held a coin minted by the emperor when this book was written. As we have often seen with these images, Jesus chooses symbols that apparently have significance to both pagan and Christian culture. He combines these again and again to produce images that have fascinating layered meanings.

Around the time Revelation was written, the emperor Domitian was in the process of deifying not just himself, but members of his family. He had already proclaimed his wife a goddess. Then he minted a coin showing her on one side, and on the other his new son surrounded by seven stars. John may have been holding one of these common coins as he wrote. So what did the imagery on the coin mean?

Coin minted during Domitian's reign, showing the emperor's son surrounded by seven stars to symbolize his deity

The seven classical "stars" were the heavenly objects visible to the naked eyes of the Romans: the sun, moon, and the five planets Mercury, Venus, Mars, Jupiter, and Saturn. Controlling these seven meant you ruled the heavens. These coins showed the boy at the center of the known universe, meaning that he was ruler of the heavens as the son of the divine Domitian, a son of god. Jesus is apparently saying here, "Domitian and his son are not the ones who rule the universe; My Father and I rule. Just as the seven churches are in my hand, so are the heavens themselves."

≡ APPLY IT

Where are you leaving something you assume is a strength completely unguarded? How can you improve that situation? Is there a gap between reputation and reality in your spiritual life?

I challenge you to say, "Jesus, help me be honest enough and strong enough to hear this word from you. Show me where people think I'm okay, but my reality does not match my reputation."

30

WELL, THERE'S YOUR TROUBLE: YOU'RE DEAD

The Queen Mary was the largest ocean liner in existence when she was launched in 1936. She sailed for four decades, until she was converted into a floating hotel and tourist attraction in Long Beach, California.

During her conversion, three massive smokestacks were taken off so they could be scraped down and repainted. Made of $3/4$-inch thick steel plates, they had survived the fiercest ocean winds and waves. But as the crane hoisted the first smokestack from the ship and lowered it onto the dock, the huge stack crumbled into dust right before the amazed onlookers.

Apparently, nothing was left of the smokestack but thirty coats of paint that had been applied over the years; the metal had completely rusted away. What had appeared to be an impressive tower of strong steel was really just... paint.

In his letter to the church at Sardis, Jesus is saying that you and I can be just like those smokestacks. We can have reputations built up over many years for strength and wisdom, when in reality, we're just paint.

We are nothing but a carefully cultivated image, long after a vital relationship with God is gone.

I think this can be a problem especially for church leaders.

C.S. Lewis said,

> Anyone who has ever taught or attempted to lead others knows the tendency in all of us toward exaggerating our depth of character while treating leniently our flaws. We consciously or subconsciously put forward a better image of ourselves than really exists. The outward appearance and the inner reality (that only God, we, and our family members know) do not match. [27]

That was the problem here in Sardis. No one knew they were hollow. Except Jesus.

THE SHOCK OF MY DEATH

Imagine the first time the Sardis Christians heard these words. They'd learned that John had seen a vision of Jesus on Patmos. The Lord had words for them! They probably received a parchment with the entire Book of Revelation on it, and someone publicly read through it in front of the whole church. That means they heard all the letters that had come before theirs, so the congregation knew what Jesus had said to Ephesus, Pergamum, and the rest.

And since they had the best reputation among all the churches, I'm sure they were very excited to hear what they anticipated would be Jesus' words of praise and admiration to them. Picture that scene — and now think of the uncomfortable silence when they heard this:

> *"I know your deeds; you have a reputation of being alive, but you are dead."* REV. 3:1B NIV

---

27 C.S. Lewis, *The Four Loves*. Mariner Books, 1971.

You're dead! I'm sure some felt embarrassed and uncomfortable at that very moment. But if they were going to grow, they needed to hear some tough words. They were spiritually dead. Their faith was no longer a living, vital part of their daily lives. It was mere ritual. Lip service.

But Jesus still cares about them. That's why he says these hard but loving words to these Christians. He shows how to bring what's dead back to life. After all, he's the world expert on that.

BRINGING THE DEAD TO LIFE

And as Tom Holladay points out, this is the same way to bring any dead or dying relationship back to life. Your marriage. Your relationship with your kids. Your work relationships. You can help bring them all to life again by learning Jesus' remedy for this church's dead relationship with him.

The church at Sardis had no apparent struggles. Jesus does not mention any persecution, or internal struggles, or false teaching, or immorality. Perhaps because there was so little pressure on the Christian community here, they simply stopped growing. More on that in the next chapter.

☰ APPLY IT

Why is struggle sometimes necessary for growth?

How can you assure your continued growth even when you are not in a time of struggle?

DIGGING DEEPER

At the time these words were written, Sardis had seen its best days, but it still had a phenomenal reputation for wealth. In fact, in many ways, it is the birthplace of modern commerce and banking.

Some facts about the wealth of Sardis:

The Pactolus River that runs near the city of Sardis was the site of an ancient gold rush, much like California. Fortune hunters prospected for gold flakes here centuries before the 49ers.

There was even a legend that explained why there was such a remarkable amount of gold in the river. When the fabled King Midas bathed in its waters to rid himself of his "golden touch," his power to create gold flowed out of him and right into the stream.

And the Greek legend of the "golden fleece" supposedly originated from the ancient method of laying sheepskins in the shallows of the river to collect gold particles.

The expression, "rich as Croesus," was widely used to indicate an extremely wealthy person. Croesus was a real historical figure, and his palace was in Sardis. He was indeed spectacularly rich.

Every modern economy owes its origins to Sardis: It's the first place on earth that ever minted coins. Doing business moved from a barter system to a monetary exchange system right here.

The city flourished until it was devastated by an earthquake in 17 AD. One Roman writer described it as:

> "The greatest earthquake in human memory. Twelve cities were destroyed in one night, but the disaster was harshest to the citizens of Sardis."

Emperor Tiberias assisted with rebuilding the city. Some scholars feel that because of the citizens' indebtedness to him, the city gave itself to the cult of emperor worship.

However, its best days were behind it. Sardis had a glorious history but it was coasting on its reputation as a golden city and would never attain its former glory again.

31

WAKE UP

The first command of Jesus in this letter: Wake up!

Everyone in that church, with its city's unique history, would have understood what he meant. The attacking Persians found the sentries at Sardis asleep. And as the city's residents soon learned, if you're not awake, you're vulnerable to attack. These days we might say, "Stop living in denial. You're not okay! You're in danger."

> *"Wake up! Strengthen what remains and is about to die, for I have found your deeds unfinished in the sight of my God."* REV. 3:2 NIV

AN INCOMPLETE WORK

These words about their deeds being incomplete were probably a reference to a famous feature of the Temple of Artemis at Sardis. When I visited its ruins, our guide pointed out that some of the columns in the temple were fluted. They had beautiful vertical grooves in them, while some were the less expensive, smoother columns. This is visible evidence of a well-known fact in the ancient world. The people of Sardis could never seem to get this temple completed. Some of the columns remain unfinished.

The temple construction started and stopped over hundreds of years. By the time of Revelation, the temple still stood incomplete. Yet that didn't seem to matter to the people. It was a popular place for visiting pagan worshippers even if only half done. So the people of Sardis were unmotivated to finish it.

The half-finished temple was another reminder of the sleepy, half-committed nature of Sardis that seemed to transfer right over to the Christian population.

THE PROBLEM OF NO PROBLEMS

Strange thing about this church. Did you notice it doesn't have any of the problems that the other churches had?

Jesus doesn't mention heresy, so they're apparently not into false teaching.

He doesn't mention poverty, because they're rich.

He doesn't mention persecution, so they're not suffering.

Here's what's happened. They're their own worst enemy. They can't blame suffering, they can't blame persecution, they can't blame poverty. They're simply spiritually dead.

Jesus criticizes this church more than all the other churches. He doesn't have anything positive to say about it — except that it has a good reputation. Which is a shell!

HOW CHURCHES DIE

What does it look like when a church eventually dies? How does that even happen? Someone said that churches often go on a similar trajectory.

God the Holy Spirit works. There's a *movement*.

Then you've got to organize it, so it turns into an *organization*. Of course this doesn't mean it's dying. Organizations can have a vital, creative culture. Then if it survives for longer than a generation with any degree of success, the organization becomes an *institution*. That doesn't have to be dead either. An institution can be alive and vibrant. However, institutions are not often about pushing forward and reaching outward; they're usually about defending what they've already obtained.

Then finally it becomes a *museum*. There's no future. There's no mission. There's no passion. There's no life. The church is just a monument to the past.

POSSE OR FORTRESS

As Lyle Schaller puts it, a church can easily turn into a *fortress*, when God wants a *posse*. Fortresses have big walls to protect what's inside. They have a king and a military sense of order. They have their own little economy, so the people within the fortress never have to venture outside into relatively unsafe territory. A posse, on the other hand, is outward-focused. It has a clear mission – to round people up! In a posse, everyone is deputized to ride.

Of course at our church we do want legacy, and multiple generations, and tradition. But we want to hand our children and our children's children a living faith, not a dead set of rituals, traditions, and routines.

CHANGE IS HARD

But here's the biggest challenge when trying to keep churches alive. Every living thing changes. Dead things don't change. In a way, it's easier to be dead!

My youngest son is seventeen years old. In the past five years he's changed in remarkable ways. All living things change.

So the question for living churches is not, will there be change? The questions are: How will we handle change? How are we hoping to change? What do we want to preserve even as we change?

Do you want to be part of a movement or a museum? Do you want to be part of something that is growing and changing and messy, or something that has already died like the ruined fortress of Sardis?

THIS IS NOT ABOUT "THEM"

When you read these rebukes, be careful and remember that this is not John, this is Jesus making this analysis. These verses do not mean that you have a license to pronounce other churches dead. Some of us Christians need to repent of our self-righteousness and judgmental attitudes toward other churches. You and I need to be open and willing to personally change, and to welcome change in our own church.

And we can't just look at these historical examples and criticize the ancient people. We need to say that we're capable of the same failure. Unless we wake up. How do we do that? Jesus tells us — in the next section.

☰ APPLY IT

If Jesus told you, *"Strengthen that which remains and is about to die,"* what could he be referring to in your life now?

32

SPIRITUAL FLAB

Maybe *because* everything was easy at Sardis, no outer persecution or inner doctrinal error, they'd grown complacent. Their faith had grown flabby.

You and I need to ask: Where has my faith become flabby? In our culture we think of flab as only physical. But we can get spiritually flabby too, and for the same two reasons — we don't work out. And we don't eat right.

Like Sardis, it's pretty easy for us sometimes, isn't it? We don't have the same persecutions that many others in the world face. Our theology tends to stay solid. So our faith can grow weaker and weaker, because we don't need to work out our faith muscles as much as Christians in other parts of the world do.

When you're out of shape, the only way to get fit is to use those muscles again, and sharpen your diet.

Jesus says, *"Strengthen what remains and is about to die..."* (REV. 3:2B NIV)

Strengthen what remains. As Tom Holladay says, that's great advice for any relationship. [28]

---

28 The section on "strengthen what remains" is slightly adapted from a message preached by Tom Holladay at Saddleback Church, Orange County, Ca., February 16, 2000, accessed at saddlebackresources.com

STRENGTHEN WHAT REMAINS

Here's an example from earthly relationships: If you're in a marriage you want to bring back to life, you don't start with that thing that you're grieving about that you feel has died. You find the one place in your marriage where you have a little bit of happiness and start there. Water it. Care for it. Strengthen what remains.

Same thing in your relationship with Jesus. Ask: What can I strengthen that still brings me life?

In your spiritual life, maybe you are realizing, "I'm dying." What's the one thing that remains? Maybe it's worship for you. Maybe it's prayer. Maybe it's reading God's Word. Or volunteering. Pour yourself into that one thing that remains (focusing on Jesus and not your own effort) and watch God strengthen you like only he can. Then the life you find there will begin to spread.

So first you wake up. You stop the denial. Then you strengthen what remains. And the next step may be the most challenging — yet the most important.

≡ APPLY IT

What do you still enjoy in your spiritual life right now? Pour yourself into that.

33

PREACH THE GOSPEL
TO YOURSELF

We're looking at words from Jesus himself about how to revitalize a spiritual life that's virtually dead. And today's words are key. They're about your mental diet.

> *"Remember what you heard and believed at first; hold to it firmly."* REV. 3:3A NLT

Once again, just as in the other letters, Jesus is not asking these Christians to do anything new or secret or extraordinary. No "Christ Plus" teaching here, no magic instant fix.

Just get back to basics — the gospel you believed at first. As Tim Keller often says, the most important thing Christians can do for their spiritual growth is to keep preaching the gospel — to themselves.

When Jesus says, *"hold to it firmly,"* he's telling us to grasp the gospel and preach it to ourselves again and again. It's so easy for us to slip away from the love of God for us.

CATCHING THE BREEZE

In my experience, it's like being in a sailboat sitting powerless in the middle of the bay. When you preach the gospel of grace to yourself again, you're raising the sails. I don't know exactly how it happens, but things start to change. You put up the sails and God breathes direction and energy into your life — and you start skidding across the bay.

"Repent and turn to me again." REV. 3:3A NLT

Remember, the word "repent" is *metanoia*, literally a "change of mind" that leads to our whole lives turning around, heading in a different direction. When we let our imaginations be captured again by the beauty of the one who died and lives again, the one whose shed blood freed us, we are spun into a new and vital direction.

SOMETIMES I JUST WANT TO STAY DEAD

But here's the problem. Sometimes, if we're honest with ourselves, we don't want to "repent and turn" to him again.

We don't *want* to be revitalized. We're afraid of change. We *like* the way things are *now*. Being dead is peaceful! Cemeteries are such quiet, restful places. If I start getting excited about God again, where will that lead? Back out into busy streets and messy situations and real life.

If I'm really honest, to return to the boat metaphor, I'm paddling as fast as I can with my own hands in the direction *I* want to go. And I'm scared to death that if I raised those sails, and turned my mind toward God and his grace again, God's going to move me in an entirely different direction. And he probably is. Because he's got far better plans for your life than you could imagine.

Listen. God's never going to ask you to do anything that won't at some point bring fulfillment and joy into your life. It will involve challenge. It will stretch you. *But that's part of being alive.* When you let God drive your life, you'll never regret it.

And it's important to start soon. As we'll see in the next chapter.

☰ APPLY IT

Ask yourself: What do I need to remember about what I heard and believed at first?

How can I "preach the gospel to myself"?

DIGGING DEEPER

A large Sardis synagogue was discovered by chance in 1962 during excavations by Harvard and Cornell Universities. It measures over 300 feet in length, the largest ancient synagogue ever found. It has elaborate, expensive, beautiful mosaic floors. It's right inside the grounds of the spectacular gymnasium and bathhouse structure in the heart of the city. Its size, wealth, and favored location speak to the prosperity and status of the Jews in Sardis during Roman times.

The lack of any mention of persecution of either Jews or Christians in Sardis reflects the secure position of the city's large Jewish community. Evidently Christians and Jews coexisted peacefully with each other and the city establishment.

It's rather ironic that Jesus told this wealthy, secure church that it was "dead." But maybe that's one of the reasons the members declined. With no obvious political, cultural, or social opponents, the Christians in Sardis had no pressing need to run to the Scripture or to prayer for answers. They never got thirsty, so they never dug a well.

The synagogue at Sardis

34

THE CLOCK IS TICKING

There's a warning at the end of verse three. And it's this: The clock is ticking.

> *"If you don't wake up, I will come to you suddenly, as unexpected as a thief."* REV. 3:3B

You know why Jesus tells you and me with such urgency to wake up?

Have you ever raised a teenager? If so, you have probably experienced the difficulty of getting one out of bed in the morning. Sometimes the only way is to give a countdown! Wake up now, or there will be consequences. That's what Jesus is saying here.

When Jesus says he will come *"suddenly, like a thief..."* it's a picture of those enemy soldiers crawling into the Sardis fortress like cat burglars while the guards slept. The reputation of that great city was never the same again. Pride led to its downfall. One day Jesus will remove this church from its place of leadership — if it does not begin to match its reputation. The clock is ticking.

And you know what? The alarm clock always goes off sooner than you think. If you are thinking, *I'm going to keep getting away with this*, there's a clock that's ticking. If you are thinking, *God's giving me more time to get my life straight,* there's a clock ticking. If you are thinking, *There's no rush,* there's a clock ticking, and every moment is one moment closer to your own day of reckoning.

The point is, if your spiritual vitality, or some other relationship, is dying, don't put off action until it is too late.

Jesus says, in effect, "Look out! Life changes more quickly than you realize. Take care of what's dying before it's gone."

DO IT NOW

So what's God telling you to do that you haven't done? Where's God telling you to turn around that you haven't turned around? The only reason he wants you to do that is because he loves you, and he has a new, better direction for your life.

Remember Jesus is directing these comments to a *church,* not only to individual Christians – although of course there is individual application here.

When churches don't change, they can die. It happened in our own church history. Our first church building was an old Victorian chapel, and after over 30 years of service, it closed down. The congregation didn't move; it just closed up shop. The building was boarded up. They didn't hold a single service for many years. The Victorian façade still looked pretty, but there was no life inside.

Other churches might keep having services, but they're just as dead as our church was at that time. It's been said about those churches, "They're mild-mannered people meeting in mild-mannered ways striving to be more mild-mannered."

But someone found a pulse in our church when it was presumed dead, and by God's grace it was fired up again. Its doors reopened. And this is important to remember too.

While Jesus says to Sardis that their church is dead right now, he also gives them hope that there's a spark of life.

So what about Sardis? Did the church heed Jesus' words and come back to life? We'll find out next.

≡ APPLY IT

Ask God right now to breathe life back into anything that is in danger of dying in your life — your spiritual life, your relationships, your passion for the gospel.

35

THE PROMISE

E ver wonder what happened to these Christians at Sardis? Did they heed what Jesus said?

According to early Christian writings, a man named Clement, trained by the Apostle Paul himself, became the first pastor here. The second pastor, Melito, served for an amazing 70 years! Eventually Sardis became a center for Christianity and until about 1071 the archbishop here supervised 27 other churches. 1,000 years of vital church ministry — I'd call that a successful turnaround!

The believers here apparently responded with enthusiasm as they heard the hope in this verse:

> "Yet you have a few people in Sardis who have not soiled their clothes. They will walk with me, dressed in white, for they are worthy." REV. 3:4 NIV

Jesus says that they will wear white. This seems to have had two meanings. First it symbolized the fact that their sins have all been washed away by Jesus. Remember Isaiah's words?

> "Come now, let us reason together," says the Lord, "though your sins be as scarlet, they shall be as white as snow." ISAIAH 1:18 NIV

White clothes had additional meaning in Roman culture. Romans wore a pure white toga on holidays, especially at triumph parades held to celebrate a great military victory.

So Jesus is not only saying that your past sins can be wiped away, but that you can be absolutely victorious over all the challenges facing your spiritual life. You will be part of the victory parade he leads over all the oppressive governments like Rome — and over all oppression and suffering in general. It's a peek into an exciting future that awaits the faithful.

Jesus is really saying to the whole church here, "If you come to me, I'm not going to berate you, I'm not going to harm you, I'm going to cleanse you. And give you a wonderful future." And this is also an invitation from Jesus to you and me.

THE BOOK OF LIFE

And there's more assurance. Jesus says of the overcomer: *"I will never blot out his name from the Book of Life..."*

A book that registered all the names of a kingdom's citizens would have been a familiar idea to the original readers of this letter. There are numerous references in ancient Roman writings to books containing the names of a city's citizens. Sardis itself, as the Western capital of the Persian and Seleucid empires, housed the archives of such books going back for centuries. We know that in some cities, like Athens, names of convicted criminals would be deleted from the books. [29]

A lot of believers wonder, "Will my name ever be deleted? Am I going to lose this salvation somehow?" Notice the way Jesus puts it. He says, "I will never" — and that word used for "never" is the strongest negative in the Greek language. It could be translated, "I will never, ever, ever blot out your name from the Book of Life."

---

29 Hemer, p. 148

And he says another reassuring thing: *"...but will acknowledge his name before my Father and his angels."* (REV. 3:5B NIV)

Jesus is saying, when you stand in glory with your entire record exposed for everybody to see, he will look at you and say, "You are mine."

Here's the promise: *Jesus will never reject you.* He will never let you go. If your spiritual life is not where he wants it to be, he loves you and wants you to change, so he writes you these love letters. If you don't change he will discipline you. But he will not reject you. He *loves* you.

And his love letter closes with the phrase, *"He who has an ear, let him hear what the spirit says to the churches."* (REV. 3:6 NIV)

That just means, this is in the Bible for you to apply to *yourself.* Sometimes we miss that. We think, *Very sad about Sardis! Hope they got their act together.* So Jesus repeats seven times, at the end of each letter, this is for you to apply to your *own* life! If you have ears, listen to what he says to these churches!

So let's finish where we started this section on Sardis. Ask yourself: Is there a gap between reputation and reality in *my* spiritual life?

≡ APPLY IT

Ask God in prayer: Help me to see and close the gaps in my life. Thank you for your love for me. Thank you for never letting me go. Thank you for loving me enough to say something about this. Please bring me back to life.

Ruins of Byzantine-era Church of St. Jean in ancient Philadelphia

THE SIXTH LETTER

36

STABILITY IN A
SHAKY WORLD

I walk through a narrow gate set into ancient brick walls. A tiny, clumsily lettered sign reads "St. Jean Church." In a single city-block-sized vacant lot stand the last remains of the once glorious Byzantine church here in Philadelphia (Not the Philadelphia in Pennsylvania but the original Philadelphia, now known as Alasehir in modern Turkey).

Massively thick columns made of local brick once held up vast arches that stretched toward the sky and supported the beautiful domed ceiling of the cathedral. The few surviving Byzantine-era churches, like the one now known as Hagia Sophia in Istanbul, help me appreciate what was lost.

Scattered around the church ruins are small sarcophagi and headstones with inscriptions bearing the names, in Latin or Arabic, of some of the believers who worshipped here and here were laid to rest.

As I explore the ruins, the minaret located directly across the street begins a loudly amplified Muslim call to prayer. Local middle school boys gather at the gate and begin jeering, swearing at our group in the few English words they know. The guide yells at them, shooing them away, but it helps me appreciate to some small degree the pressure the local Christians have been under as the vastly outnumbered minority religion for the last several centuries. Yet despite all the upheaval, and against great odds, a Christian population does remain here, encouraged, no doubt, by what Jesus said to them in this letter.

BUILT FOR MISSIONARY WORK

The city here was established in 189 BC by King Eumenes II of Pergamum. He named the city in honor of his beloved brother, who would be his successor, Attalus II (*Phila delphos* literally means "brotherly love").

Philadelphia was planted where the borders of the ancient kingdoms of Mysia, Lydia and Phrygia met, and was chosen because of this strategic geography. It was founded specifically as a missionary city.

Not for Christian missionaries; they were to come later. It was begun as part of a mission to expand Greek culture. The idea was that travelers on their way home from business trips would find a hospitable place to stay, and would become so enamored of Greek music, theater, religion and philosophy that they would carry it home.

And it worked. The Philadelphians were so successful that by 19 AD citizens of the nearby Lydian kingdom had forgotten their own language and were almost entirely Greek in language and customs.

The city itself wasn't much — but it was designed to spread the seed of Greek thought to the rest of the world. And so the Christians were a marked minority in this city, persecuted by the Greeks of the city who were evangelists of Hellenistic religious thought, and saw Christianity as a competing belief system.

In addition, there was a large group of "Judaizers," Christians in the synagogue who believed that Greek converts to Christianity also had to convert to the Jewish religion in its strictest form, and adopt all of the Jewish religious customs and rituals — circumcision and a kosher diet, for example.

It was a volatile cultural mix.

WHOLE LOT OF SHAKING

Earthquakes also hammered Philadelphia. The city was nearly destroyed by a quake in 17 AD. It was a disaster remembered in accounts that have survived to this day as "the greatest earthquake in human history".[30] The devastation to the city was so severe that the Roman Senate not only offered rebuilding assistance, but also exempted the city from its federal taxes for the next five years.

Philadelphia continued to be hit by major and minor quakes and aftershocks throughout the first century.

Ancient writers tell us how every time an aftershock hit, people ran out of the buildings, all the way into the countryside, because the buildings were held up by giant pillars that would sway and collapse. In fact, Philadelphia experienced so many aftershocks that most of the remaining residents eventually just lived outdoors entirely. They no longer felt safe living under a roof, since they had seen so many buildings collapse! Again, the Roman writer Strabo records, "The actual town has few inhabitants, for the majority live in the countryside. One is surprised even at the few, that they are so fond of the place, when they have such insecure dwellings." [31]

So the Christians in this city were very discouraged. Persecution from the culture, persecution within their congregations, from the Judaizers, earthquakes. They were at a point where they were probably tempted to just give up.

---

30 Hemer, p. 156

31 Ibid.

Did they? Well, we know from history exactly what happened to them. And I'll tell you the rest of their story in just a few pages.

But first, in these verses, Jesus gives three promises for those who feel discouraged. If you feel shaken by the quakes of your life lately, read this:

> "Write this letter to the angel of the church in Philadelphia.
>
> "This is the message from the one who is holy and true,
>> the one who has the key of David.
>
> "What he opens, no one can close;
>> and what he closes, no one can open:
>
> "I know all the things you do, and I have opened a door for you that no one can close. You have little strength, yet you obeyed my word and did not deny me. Look, I will force those who belong to Satan's synagogue — those liars who say they are Jews but are not — to come and bow down at your feet. They will acknowledge that you are the ones I love.
>
> "Because you have obeyed my command to persevere, I will protect you from the great time of testing that will come upon the whole world to test those who belong to this world. I am coming soon. Hold on to what you have, so that no one will take away your crown. All who are victorious will become pillars in the Temple of my God, and they will never have to leave it. And I will write on them the name of my God, and they will be citizens in the city of my God — the new Jerusalem that comes down from heaven from my God. And I will also write on them my new name.
>
> "Anyone with ears to hear must listen to the Spirit and understand what he is saying to the churches." REV. 3:7-13 NLT

It's interesting to me that the only thing left of the ancient church at Philadelphia today are giant pillars! Jesus told the church that they would become "pillars in the temple of my God, and they will never have to leave it." We'll decode that later.

Do you ever feel shaky, insecure, under fire? Have you experienced so much turmoil and heartache from the earthquakes of life that you are afraid to live "under a roof" so to speak, in relationships with others and in a community of faith?

As we discover insights into these ancient words of Jesus to the Philadelphians, you'll find yourself inspired and uplifted too!

≡ APPLY IT

How have metaphorical "earthquakes" in your life — of failure or relational wounds or grief, for example — impacted you?

37

TO BOLDLY GO

"I have opened a door for you that no one can close (though) you have little strength..." REV. 3:8

One of my favorite authors and speakers, Doug Fields, asks, "Have you ever noticed that the human race is divided into two types of people? This has been scientifically proven. Those who love classic Star Trek and those who are wrong." [32]

I definitely fall into the "love classic Star Trek" category. But no matter what category you fall into, almost everybody knows the phrase at the beginning of the show. If you're a Klingon, or you grew up in a cave, let me explain. In Star Trek there's a group of people exploring outer space and they have been put on a mission:

"...to boldly go where no man has gone before."

As Doug says, I think this is how God made us to live. To boldly go! I believe we all start out this way. When we're kids, we want to be challenged and we want adventure and we want to be heroes.

---

32 This and other quotes in this section from Doug Fields, *"When You're Discouraged,"* sermon preached at Saddleback Church, Orange County, Ca., December 4–5, 2004 accessed at saddleback-resources.com

Our youngest son David is a teenager now, and still loves space adventures and superhero movies. But I remember how as a child he was constantly pretending to be a hero. If he wasn't Batman, he was Obi-Wan Kenobi. If he wasn't Spider-Man, he was pretending to be a firefighter. Or a policeman. Or a pastor (just kidding about that last one).

This wonderful drive we have "to boldly go" unfortunately gets wiped out for many of us by a killer disease called *discouragement*. At some point in our lives, we've had so many doors slammed in our faces that we stop boldly going.

What are you discouraged about right now? Something to do with work? Seemingly unanswered prayer? Family issues? Finances? Illness? Unconquered sin? Loneliness?

Eighty-three times in the Bible, God says, "Do not be discouraged" or "Do not fear" or a combination of the two.

THE EFFECTS OF DISCOURAGEMENT

Why is God so concerned about discouragement? Because it keeps you from going boldly into your life in three ways:

· **Discouragement can make me blind to opportunity.**

Someone said that living with discouragement is like driving a car while looking only in the rear view mirror. You look back at all your mistakes. You look back at all the ways things used to be better. And you don't notice the direction signs right in front of you.

You start saying things about your future like, "I'll *never...*" Finish the sentence. "Be a good father." "Be a good mother." "Be a good student." "Get married." "Get a job." "Get sober." And your own discouragement becomes a self-fulfilling prophecy.

· Discouragement can make me vulnerable to weakness.

Think about it. When you give in to temptation, chances are pretty high that you're discouraged. To paraphrase Doug Fields again, when you ate that box of donuts and that gallon of ice cream and consumed that tin of See's peanut brittle this week, you were probably discouraged that your prune juice and raw oat diet wasn't working.

When you're discouraged, four very destructive words come into play: *"I might as well."* I might as well eat that. I might as well drink that. I might as well buy that. I might as well click on that web site. I might as well.... And the list goes on.

Then, when you give *in* to that temptation, do you feel better? Of course not. It's a vicious cycle. You're discouraged, so you give in to temptation, so you're more discouraged.

· Discouragement can prevent me from seeing my own worth.

There was an article in *The New York Times* about a man named John Byrnes. It describes him as alcoholic and homeless, living on the streets of New York.

One day he sees a fire consuming a building. People are trapped. And John catches a 2-year-old baby whose desperate mother threw her from a window. It hits the national media. But when he's interviewed, in a discouraged tone, he says, "I ain't no hero. I'm just a drunken bum."

He did something amazing! But he's been discouraged for so long that even after doing something great, he can't see his worth — and describes himself as a drunken bum.

You may be thinking, *Great story, René. But my discouragement hasn't left me homeless.* I wonder. I wonder if your discouragement affects your moods so much people don't want to be around you. I wonder if your discouragement steals your joy and leaves you critical and negative. Most important, I wonder if your discouragement keeps you from going boldly through the open doors God puts right in front of you.

The good news is this: There are three promises in this letter from Jesus to the Philadelphians that relate to each of these three dangers.

In the meantime, listen to Jesus when he says, *"Hold on to what you have..."* Hold on. Don't give up. Better days are ahead. Look for the doors Jesus will open for you.

☰ APPLY IT

Have you been discouraged lately? In what ways? Ask God to speak to you through the letter to the Philadelphians.

38

THE KEY THAT UNLOCKS
EVERY DOOR

The first promise in his letter to the Philadelphians: *Jesus replaces closed doors with open doors.*

Maybe you've seen doors slam in your face lately: The door to a new job. The door to marriage. The door to having a child. The main sound effect in your life lately has been Slam. Slam. Slam. And you're afraid of how much another slammed door would hurt.

This church must have felt that too. But Jesus says:

> *"These are the words of him who is holy and true, who holds the key of David. What he opens no one can shut, and what he shuts, no one can open. I know your deeds. See, I have placed before you an open door that no one can shut."* REV. 3:7,8 NIV

THE ONE WHO STAYS TRUE

Let's do some decoding. The people of Philadelphia — not just the Christians, but all the people — were feeling betrayed by the government. We know from history that the emperor Domitian had ordered all the vineyards of Philadelphia to be torn up by the roots. Why? Because the Philadelphians had a reputation as the best winemakers in the world, and Domitian wanted the vineyards of Rome to have that claim to fame. So he ordered the Philadelphian vineyards destroyed and devastated the local economy.

There was naturally a deep distrust of authority and sense of betrayal. I think that's one of the reasons Jesus calls himself, *"the one who is holy and true."* That means he will not betray us. He will *stay true.* We can count on him.

And he has given us *"an open door."*

OPEN DOORS

Perhaps you've seen God as the God of *closed* doors. The one who always says no. Or maybe you see him as the God of the *trap* doors. You're always expecting something to go wrong. But God is the God of the *open* door.

What does that mean? The "open door" is a metaphor for opportunity. It's used several times like this in the Bible. In 1 Corinthians 16, Paul is writing to the church at Corinth and says, *"I will stay in Ephesus ...a wide door for effective work is open to me..."* (1 COR. 16:9 NIV). The same metaphor is in 2 Corinthians 2:12: *"When I came to Troas to proclaim the good news... a door was open for me..."* To the Colossians, Paul writes, *"Pray that God will give me an open door for the word..."* (COL. 4:3 NIV). An open door stands for an opportunity to be used by God to spread his Word.

So when Jesus says: *"See, I have placed before you an open door that no one can shut,"* here's what I think it meant for this church. Remember, Philadelphia was on the border of three countries. Jesus is saying, in effect, look at that open door! Followers of Alexander the Great built your city to spread Greek culture, but I see it as a door for the good news of the gospel.

Let's decode another phrase in this verse. What does it mean when Jesus says he *"holds the key of David"*? Jesus is referring to a verse from the book of Isaiah: *"I will place on his shoulder the key of the house of David. He shall open and no one shall shut. He shall shut and no one shall open."* (Isaiah 22:22 NIV)

In its original context this referred to a man of integrity who would soon replace a corrupt court official in Isaiah's time. He was literally the gatekeeper to the city, the palace, and the temple. But over the centuries this verse came to be understood as an apt description of the coming Messiah. The Messiah would have the keys to Jerusalem and the Temple. In other words, he would be the way into the city of God and the presence of God, including the Holy of Holies.

THE GIGANTIC KEY

To our modern ears it sounds funny to hear Isaiah say, *"I'll place on his shoulder the key."* But in those days, keys were much, much bigger than keys are today.

And here's my chance to brag on something no one cares about from my past, but I'll mention anyway: When I was in high school, I was awarded the key to the city of San Jose from Mayor Janet Grey Hayes for some high school accomplishment. She brought out this massive styrofoam gold key for the picture. You've seen these ceremonial keys. Well, I was very disappointed to find out that I was not allowed to take the giant key home from the ceremony. Instead, I was given a tiny little keepsake key in a ring box. I remember thinking, *What a rip-off!* I wanted to put that giant key on my key ring and nonchalantly brag on myself that way. Imagine it: "Lemme get my keys. What? What is this, you ask? This giant, three yard-long key? Oh, just a little something THE MAYOR AWARDED ME!"

Well, back in Old Testament days, the keys really *were* that big (People must have lost them much less frequently than I lose mine today!). In those days the key to the city really did unlock the gate to the *whole city.*

With this background in mind, look at this verse again: *"What he opens no one can shut, and what he shuts no one can open."* That means no human being and no set of circumstances in this world can keep you from accomplishing what Christ asks you to do. He holds the gigantic key that can unlock every massive gate.

Just one example: The Romans thought they had the Apostle John all locked up. They put him in chains on the remote island of Patmos. But Jesus opened a door.

He gave John a vision, and John wrote down this very book, the Book of Revelation — and 1,900 years later, long after Greece and Rome have fallen, long after the Roman rulers who locked him away are forgotten, John's ministry is still very much alive to this day.

Because when you walk through the open door that Jesus sets before you, *no one* can shut the door. Not even Caesar.

MOVE TOWARD THE DOOR

What is the door of opportunity that God has in front of you right now? Maybe it's an open door to a fresh start. Maybe it's an open door of evangelism. There's somebody in your neighborhood or somebody at your work who needs a follower of Jesus to love him or her. Maybe it's a ministry opportunity. Maybe it's a new job that will stretch you. Maybe it's a relationship. Walk toward that door with confidence.

Perhaps you're uncertain because all the details of this new opportunity aren't completely settled: What if it's not an open door after all? Brother Andrew, an Eastern European pastor who used to smuggle Bibles into communist countries, once said,

> God's open doors work like the automatic doors at grocery stores. You figure out what you believe God wants you to do,

then move toward the door. If it's God's will, as you begin to move toward it, God opens it. But if you never move toward it, you'll never know.

Are you boldly going where you believe Jesus wants you to go?

Maybe you're still discouraged. You're thinking, *I don't know if I'm strong enough.* Next, Jesus has another promise for you in this letter.

≡ APPLY IT

What is an open door Jesus seems to be placing before you? Are you hesitant to approach it? Why?

39

HIS STRENGTH FOR
YOUR WEAKNESS

The second promise in this letter: *Jesus will replace your weakness with strength.*

Maybe you're exhausted. You've been working so hard. You feel like you've given it your all — and it's not enough! And what Jesus says to you is, "I know."

> *"I know that you have little strength, yet you have kept my word and have not denied my name."* REV. 3:8 NIV

Jesus knows. He knows. And he promises his strength.

> *"Since you have kept my command to endure patiently, I will also keep you from the hour of trial that is going to come upon the whole world to test those who live on the earth. I am coming soon. Hold on to what you have, so that no one will take your crown."*
> REV. 3:10,11 NIV

Please don't misunderstand what Jesus was saying to Christians about suffering. This church had already been through a time of battering. You could tell from the tone of this letter, this church had really been hammered. So Jesus is not saying that good Christians are immune from suffering.

He's saying the Philadelphians will be protected from a time of suffering that will come upon the rest of the Roman world. What could this mean? We know from history that even the worst of the Roman persecutions were not uniformly enforced across the empire. For various reasons, local officials did not always carry out Rome's commands to arrest or execute Christians. Apparently the Philadelphians were spared from one of the horrific future persecutions that the rest of the cities would need to endure.

And remember, even for the Christians that would have to endure the hour of trial, Jesus promises that he will hold them up. And that's true for all of us.

Maybe you are worrying right now.

Worrying about the future.

Worrying about the wars in the world.

Worrying about terrorism.

Worrying about your kids.

Jesus says to this church – and to you – I will give you strength. He says to them, *"The one who overcomes I will make a pillar in the temple of my God. Never again will he leave it."* (REV. 3:12A NIV)

SAFE AND STABLE

Remember how the earthquakes of that region would knock the pillars of all their buildings down? Jesus says, *"I'll make you a pillar in the temple of my God,"* meaning you will become a pillar that will never fall. He will give you stability.

Then he says, *"Never again will he leave it."* Remember how ancient Philadelphia experienced so many aftershocks that the remaining residents eventually just lived outdoors? They no longer felt safe living under a roof, and were tired of running outside all the time!

But Jesus says, "Never again will he leave this temple." This sounds like a promise specifically directed to people who did not trust the indoors anymore. Jesus is saying to them, one day, you won't have to run outside anymore. No more fear. He will lead you to safety.

But the third promise is the best of all. That's next.

☰ APPLY IT

Where do you feel weak right now? Ask God to strengthen you. Remind yourself that he will make you into a pillar that will never fall!

40

A BRAND NEW NAME

A nd finally, a third promise: *Jesus replaces rejection with respect.*

The church at Philadelphia was being rejected by everyone, but what really hurt was when they were rejected by other religious believers.

This next verse may be a little confusing:

> *"I will make those who are of the synagogue of Satan — who claim to be Jews though they are not, but are liars — I will make them come and fall down at your feet and acknowledge that I have loved you."* REV. 3:9 NIV

Now wait a minute. Is this an anti-Semitic statement? Who is this "synagogue of Satan" crowd? It helps to recall the difficulty faced by the church at Smyrna from the local synagogue there. There was a rift developing in some Jewish congregations about what to do with the Christ-followers among them. Some synagogues were turning Christians over to the Roman authorities in an ultimately vain effort to placate Caesar. Most commentators believe this verse refers to these tensions. In addition, the phrase *"I will make them... acknowledge I have loved you"* suggests leaders in the local synagogue were also part of the group known as "the Judaizers." These people misrepresented both Christianity and Judaism.

Judaizers believed in "Christ Plus" theology. They were believers in Jesus as the Messiah but also they tied to salvation all the ceremony and ritual of traditional orthodox Judaism, like kosher food laws and circumcision. They were saying to the Christians at Philadelphia, as they said to the Christians in Galatia, "We're the ones God truly loves — and not you, because we keep all the Jewish rules to perfection!"

There is nothing more discouraging than having the supposed experts tell you that you stink. Jesus is saying that one day they will recognize, *"I have loved you."*

When you are rejected by other religious people, by family members, by friends, by authorities at work, remember that someone so much greater loves you.

LOVED AND ACCEPTED

Remember the lunch tables in junior high? All the cool kids got to sit at the cool kids' table. And the rest of us kind of hoped we'd be asked to join them one day.

Well, the Christians at Philadelphia were never invited to the cool kids' table. Not the cool kids of religion, not the cool kids of society. They were rejected. In fact, they were driven out from their synagogue and their town again and again.

And Jesus says to them:

> *"I will write on him the name of my God and the name of the city of my God, the New Jerusalem, which is coming down out of heaven from my God; and I will also write on him my new name."* REV. 3:12B NIV

What's all this about names?

The point is, your whole life people write names on you. Maybe you were called names in school. I was. Schlaep-rock. Clumsy. Oaf. And those were from my friends!

Some of you heard the names too. And no one sees them, but they are written on you to this day, like graffiti. Names like: Loser. Fatso. Klutz. And when you're discouraged, you remember the graffiti. Not only that — some of you are grabbing a can of spray paint and writing graffiti on yourself. Idiot. Has-been. Failure.

Jesus says, let me wipe off that graffiti so you can see what I've engraved on you. Names like: Beloved. Treasure. Jewel. Cherished child of grace.

See past the ugly spray paint to the words Jesus has engraved on you. Don't let defeat define you. Let God define you.

≡ APPLY IT

Thank God today that he has called you his own beloved child! Ask him to help you see the names of love he etches on your soul.

41

WHEN YOU ARE
DISCOURAGED

If you really want to end your discouragement today, you cannot miss the wisdom in this final phrase. It's a phrase you see a lot in *The Seven.* Are you getting it?

> *"He who has an ear, let him hear what the Spirit says to the churches."* REV. 3:13 NIV

Two key questions to ask when you feel discouraged:

1. Who am I listening to?

The liars or the Lord? If you listen to negative people, then you're going to feel negative. But if you listen to what God has to say about you, you're going to be lifted up.

That's why the Bible is so important. Maybe you've thought of it just as a history book. Maybe no one has ever explained to you that the Bible is God's love letter to you.

"...hear what the Spirit says"!

God says there's an open door.

God says you are of immeasurable worth to him.

God says you are his son. You are his daughter.

There are beautiful positive promises throughout the Bible for you, so get into the Word and learn it.

2. Am I looking at the closed doors or the open doors?

It's interesting that Jesus says, *"See, I have set before you an open door."* He doesn't just say, *"I have set before you an open door."* He says: *"See it!"* The word can be translated, *"Behold!"* It's in a verb tense that means not just one time. It means, *keep beholding!*

Are you always looking for open doors – or do you just blunder past them?

Maybe you are so focused on the closed doors, and so sure there are no open doors, you are literally locking doors. You go home and hide out from people. You have a pity party, pull the curtains, and watch a depressing movie.

When you're hiding out like that it's a strong indication that you're seeing only locked doors.

Ask God to help you locate the open doors, and rediscover your sense of mission.

Did the Philadelphian church walk through the door or stay behind? Find out next.

☰ APPLY IT

Are you praying for open doors? When you wake up tomorrow, pray, "God, please open some doors for me today!"

42

STANDING STRONG

This little letter to the Philadelphians is a nice pep talk from Jesus — but did it work?

Here's the rest of the story. This message must have strengthened the church at Philadelphia because history records that for centuries, when many of the churches we've already studied about in Revelation had failed or faded away, Christians were still present in Philadelphia.

Seemingly without power, this church withstood the massive Ottoman assault, the vast Crusader waves that swept over this region, and stood strong as a missionary-sending church well into the Middle Ages. Some church historians trace much of the early Christian missionary work in India to a group of ministers sent by this church at Philadelphia.

In fact, Philadelphia was the last Greek-speaking Christian stronghold in inner Asia Minor. Its Greek inhabitants fled the town during World War I and created New Philadelphia in Greece, although there are still some Turkish-speaking Christian congregations here.

They didn't look like much when this letter was written. But their triumphant story had just begun.

Your life may not look like much right now. But your story is not over. There is still time for you to boldly go where God has opened doors.

≡ APPLY IT

Pray: "God thank you for today, another day to be alive, a day to boldly go ahead into the life that you've given me."

Recently excavated street in ancient Laodicean shopping district.
Grooves worn by chariot and wagon wheels are visible in the paving
stones, evidence of the heavy commercial traffic through this wealthy city.

THE SEVENTH LETTER

43

TO SELF-SATISFIED PEOPLE

Did you know that you are probably one of the richest people in the world?

If you own a home, you are in the top 3% of the world's income level.

If you own a car, you are in the top 6%.

The average American is twice as rich — even adjusting for inflation — than in 1957.

But there's a big difference between having a rich lifestyle and living a truly rich life. That's what Jesus explains to the Christians in Laodicea in the final of the seven letters.

At the time this letter was written, Laodicea was the richest of all the cities in the huge Roman province of Asia Minor, richer by far than any of the cities we have read about in this book.

ON TOP OF THE WORLD

The Laodiceans were literally looking down on the world. Their city sat on a nearly square plateau right above the junction of two major trade routes that funneled through a narrow valley. So it became a business hub.

Then the Laodiceans developed special black wool that was famously soft and glossy, and was eagerly sought after in the ancient world because it was treated by Laodicean textile experts with a waxy dye that made it ideal for water-resistant garments called *trimata*. Laodicean black wool was the go-to material for cold, rainy days.

Because of this prized export and the trade route, money poured into the region, and the Laodiceans leveraged that even further by becoming the primary banking center of the region.

Later Laodicea also developed a famous medical school, which developed a treatment for eye conditions. This eye balm became another claim to fame for the city.

As I walk onto the Laodicean plateau, our guide Tulu tells me that only a few years ago this was nothing but a field covered with wild flowers. Then the excavations began. And spectacular ruins are now emerging from centuries of rubble. There are vast theaters, waterworks, fountains, temples, beautifully paved streets, and gorgeous homes. All this wealth was abandoned, buried, and forgotten, long after this city seemed to rule the world.

WE DON'T NEED A THING

In the previous section, I mentioned the devastating earthquake of 17 AD. Laodicea experienced that too, and then another massive quake in 60 AD. But by this time they were so wealthy that, when the government of Rome offered financial assistance for the city's rebuilding, the Laodiceans refused! They wanted to remain as financially independent from Rome as possible. They were the only city destroyed by the earthquake to turn down government assistance.

Tacitus, who was a Roman senator and historian, wrote:

Laodicea rose from ruins by the strength of her own resources, and with no help from us. [33]

Textiles, pharmaceuticals, banking, political neutrality – Laodicea was the Switzerland of Asia Minor.

And it's to this church that Jesus says:

> "Write this letter to the angel of the church in Laodicea. This is the message from the one who is the Amen — the faithful and true witness, the beginning of God's new creation:
>
> "I know all the things you do, that you are neither hot nor cold. I wish that you were one or the other! But since you are like lukewarm water, neither hot nor cold, I will spit you out of my mouth!
>
> "You say, 'I am rich. I have everything I want. I don't need a thing!' And you don't realize that you are wretched and miserable and poor and blind and naked.
>
> "So I advise you to buy gold from me — gold that has been purified by fire. Then you will be rich. Also buy white garments from me so you will not be shamed by your nakedness, and ointment for your eyes so you will be able to see. I correct and discipline everyone I love. So be diligent and turn from your indifference.
>
> "Look! I stand at the door and knock. If you hear my voice and open the door, I will come in, and we will share a meal together as friends. Those who are victorious will sit with me on my throne, just as I was victorious and sat with my Father on his throne.
>
> "Anyone with ears to hear must listen to the Spirit and understand what he is saying to the churches." REV. 3:14-22 NLT

---

33   Hemer, p. 193

Again, you must have been able to hear a pin drop when that was first read to the Laodicean church. Surely it came as a total shock. They thought they had it all together — and that was part of their problem!

THE CHALLENGE OF COMFORT

You and I face the same challenge today. One of the greatest obstacles to continued spiritual growth in life is simply becoming too comfortable. And you know this from your own experience, right?

If there is a challenge facing me, I am on my knees, chasing after God! When things are going fine, often I'm too busy for that kind of earnest prayer. Can't always squeeze God in when the calendar's so full of important things to do!

But comfort doesn't have to lead to spiritual stagnation. Jesus does not insist that the Laodiceans move to Philadelphia or Pergamum and suffer. Jesus knows there are spiritual moves they can make that will create dynamic growth, right up there on the rich plateau of Laodicea.

You and I desperately need to know this. How can Christians in a comfortable situation avoid stagnation and self-satisfied pride, and instead continue to grow and develop into the likeness of Christ? That's next.

≡ APPLY IT

Do you think churches today need to hear Jesus' words to the Laodiceans? Why?

Can you relate to the situation of the church at Laodicea? How?

DIGGING DEEPER

The Book of Revelation isn't the only time Laodicea is mentioned in the Bible. Four times in Colossians the Apostle Paul mentions this church:

"I want you to know how much I have agonized for you and for the church at Laodicea, and for many other believers who have never met me personally." COLOSSIANS 2:1 NLT

"I can assure you that he [Epaphras] prays hard for you and also for the believers in Laodicea and Hierapolis." COL. 4:13 NLT

"Please give my greetings to our brothers and sisters at Laodicea, and to Nympha and the church that meets in her house." COL. 4:15 NLT

"After you have read this letter, pass it on to the church at Laodicea so they can read it, too. And you should read the letter I wrote to them." COL. 4:16 NLT

Archaeologists have only begun to uncover the vast ruins of Laodicea, making some fascinating discoveries.

On the main street of the city there was an extensive Nymphaneum, literally a "House of Nymphs". This was an elaborate fountain and water pumping station, similar to the fountains that many of the beautiful Greco-Roman cities built right in the center of town. These elaborate water fountains were named after the *nymphs*, Roman water-spirits thought to inhabit waterfalls and streams. They were often built under a dome with huge arches to provide shade, and benches to invite people to rest.

One fascinating discovery the excavators made when uncovering the ruins of the "House of Nympha" or water fountain in Laodicea: Part of it had, at some point, been converted into a church. This was probably some time after the New Testament era, but it's

Ruins of the church built in the Nymphaneum at Laodicea
Photo credit: Dr. Celal Şimşek/Laodikeia excavation

apparently the only nymphaneum converted to this purpose in the ancient world.[34]

Could the Laodicean Christians have built a chapel there because this Nymphaneum is the place believers regularly met to worship, pray, and study in the earliest days of the movement?

It seems to me that Paul may possibly be making a sly inside reference to this when he tells the Laodiceans to "give my greetings to our brothers and sisters at Laodicea, and to Nympha and the church that meets in her house." (COL. 4:15)

---

34 http://www.biblicalarchaeology.org/daily/biblical-topics/new-testament/laodicea-columns-reveal-the-grandeur-of-an-early-christian-center/

44

COMFORTABLY NUMB

There are a lot of dangers you could encounter in places like Africa or the Middle East and other hot spots around the globe. But Jesus warns the Laodiceans that there are different dangers in comfortable, wealthy societies.

Jesus uses an unusual characteristic of their water supply to point this out. Laodicea was on a high plateau on one side of a narrow valley. For all its riches, it lacked one crucial resource — water. There are no water springs or wells on the plateau, and even the nearby river dries up in summer.

HOT TUB TIME

Just a few miles away, easily visible across the valley, was another beautiful Greco-Roman city, Hierapolis. This community was the site of hot springs that were piped into elaborate Roman baths where people would simply sit and soak. You can still luxuriate in those very same baths today!

The water in Hierapolis bubbles out of the ground at a constant 95 degrees Fahrenheit. Rich in minerals, it spills out of wide pools over the edges of the cliff here, creating a thick curtain of white calcium carbonate stalactites 300 feet high and nearly a mile wide! The astonishing bleached cliffs are so remarkable they've been designated a World Heritage Site. They gleam in the sunshine when viewed from across the valley in Laodicea. It must have been galling for the Laodiceans to see this, like a silent boast of the abundant hot water resources at Hierapolis.

COOL CLEAR WATER

A few miles in the other direction was the city of Colossae. It was at the foot of a tall mountain range that had snow for much of the year. Pure water was a notable feature of Colossae. One ancient writer describes three mountain streams joining above the city and falling together in a beautiful double waterfall through the gorge that led to the town's water supply.

So Hierapolis had nonstop, piping hot mineral water. Colossae had abundant, ice cold, refreshing mountain water. But the Laodicean engineers had to find ways to get water pumped to their dry city.

They designed an elaborate system that piped in water from about six miles away, through clay and lead pipes, into a huge water pumping station in the middle of town. When we visited Laodicea we saw evidence of this system everywhere. Ancient water pipes littered the ground in every direction.

One problem, however.

By the time the water got to Laodicea, it was neither hot nor cold. It was lukewarm. For all their wealth, they could not buy the perfect water setup that their neighbor cities enjoyed naturally. The Laodiceans did install some expensive furnaces to heat up water for their baths, but drinking water remained tepid.

Jesus turns this situation into a spiritual analogy:

> *"I know all the things you do, that you are neither hot nor cold. I wish that you were one or the other! But since you are like*

lukewarm water, neither hot nor cold, I will spit you out of my mouth!" REV. 3:15,16 NLT

I agree with my friend Mark Spurlock's take on this. I think Jesus is saying you are not serving any purpose. Hot water is soothing. Cold water is refreshing. You're neither. You are not making a contribution. You have no passion about anything.

INDIFFERENT TO THEIR INDIFFERENCE

In 1986, Nobel Peace Prize recipient Elie Wiesel said during his acceptance speech, "The opposite of love is not hate. It's indifference. The opposite of success is not failure. It's indifference. The opposite of life is not death. It's indifference."

Indifference is living life uncommitted to any one thing in particular. And indifference can rob you of your joy in the Christian life.

As Todd Wendorff wrote, "You're cruising along in your faith and after a while you sense a dullness, a sense of apathy towards God that wasn't there before and now it is. Or maybe it's a difficulty to stay connected to God on a daily basis. You begin to drift. There's lots of things that you do, but you're not really sure of your priorities any more."

When we get too comfortable, we can become indifferent. We neglect our calling. Lose our sense of purpose. Stop plunging in to make a difference.

William Butler Yates' poem "The Second Coming," written in the aftermath of World War I, imagines the beginning of Armageddon with these haunting lines: "The best lack all conviction, while the worst / are full of passionate intensity."[35] That could have described the Laodiceans. What about us? Do we lack conviction, leaving passionate intensity to evil people?

---

35 William Butler Yeats, *The Green Helmet and Other Poems*. New York: The Macmillan Company, 1912.

Ask yourself: Am I living out my calling as a Christian? Am I eager to sacrifice in order to make a difference? *Or am I simply trying to make myself as comfortable as possible?* That's what lukewarm indifference looks like. And I have found myself there many times.

EMPTY CHURCHES

When we travelled through Turkey to visit the sites of these seven churches, we saw lots of beautiful basilicas. The great domed Hagia Sophia in Istanbul is the greatest example of early Christian architecture I have ever seen. But no church meets there anymore. It is literally a museum. The shell is there, but there's nothing living inside.

I think that is what Jesus is warning the Laodiceans about when he says, *"I am about to spit you out of my mouth"* (REV. 3:16B NIV). He is not telling them that they will lose their salvation. He is telling them their lampstand will be removed — their church will no longer have its place of prominence and influence. He's saying, you are on the verge of becoming irrelevant.

Remember, Jesus Christ is more concerned about the kind of influence churches have, and the way they represent him, than the most vocal church critic today!

But Jesus loves the church. And he loves you and me as part of his church. He calls on us, too, to leave our indifference and return to our calling before we become a relic of the past.

≡ APPLY IT

How can a comfortable life make it harder to seek God with all your heart?

Have you ever seen a church that has become a museum?

How do churches become irrelevant?

45

THE CURSE OF
CRUISE CONTROL

There's an urban legend about a man who purchased a brand new Winnebago. On a road trip to California his vehicle slowly rumbled off the road, hit some trees, and overturned. The CHP found him in the back of the RV relatively unharmed. When asked what he was doing back there, he replied, "I went back to make myself a cup of coffee after I put the RV on cruise control."

One day self-driving cars may make this a possibility, but for now, putting your car on cruise control does not mean you can stop paying attention to road hazards.

Jesus is speaking here to Christians who put their spiritual growth on cruise control. They were so comfortably distracted that they didn't even realize they were headed for a crash.

> *"You say, 'I am rich. I have everything I want. I don't need a thing!' And you don't realize that you are wretched and miserable and poor and blind and naked."* REV. 3:17 NLT

Jesus isn't just saying, "Stop being mediocre." That's the way I hear this letter sometimes applied. No, he says exactly why he is put off by this church. *"You say, I have no need of anything."* They thought they were entirely self-sufficient. They were proud. Even though they were believers, they didn't think they needed Jesus anymore. Their success led them to exclude Jesus from their daily lives in any practical sense.

ALL BY MYSELF

Remember how, after the earthquake of 60 AD, the Laodiceans refused the financial assistance of Caesar and rebuilt their city with their own money? They were the only ancient Roman city ever to refuse a Roman subsidy after an earthquake.

There are intriguing new discoveries in the recently uncovered ruins of Laodicea related to this era of rebuilding — inscriptions on buildings constructed after the earthquake. One individual, Nicostratus, rebuilt the stadium and another public building here. His inscription states proudly that he did so "out of my own resources."

A similar phrase occurs in the numerous inscriptions on public buildings rebuilt by a man named Flaccus. He paid for a furnace and pipes that heated covered walkways along the streets, and provided piped oil at the public baths. He goes on at some length in his inscriptions to describe how he did this at "great personal expense." [36]

Just as the Laodiceans refused the help of the Roman emperor after the earthquake that destroyed their city, here they are refusing the help of the Emperor of the Universe. And for the same reason. They are intensely self-sufficient, too proud to receive help of any kind from anyone.

And in a way, this is the worst kind of sin. When I am proud I don't listen to constructive criticism. I cut off the offer of help. I don't see my need for further grace from God. "No thanks! I'm good!" We love to put up inscriptions on our lives: "I did it... all by myself!" Until that becomes a lament: "I am... all by myself."

---

36 Hemer, p. 195

Even if I am a Christian, I can lose touch with the core message of the gospel. I am not only *saved* by God's grace, but I continue to *grow* by God's grace, not my own self-effort.

REALITY CHECK

So Jesus holds up a spiritual mirror that sees past all the riches of the Laodicean banking culture and the reputation of their eye medicine and finery of their clothing industry, and shows that, spiritually, they are actually the opposite of all that. They are poor and blind and naked.

He is like the little boy in the story of the emperor's new clothes. The vain emperor parades around naked, having been told by a con artist that the fabric he is wearing is so expensive it is only visible to people of truly refined taste. No one is willing to state the obvious, because no one wants to admit they don't see his clothes, until a small child shouts out, "The emperor has no clothes!"

It's so easy to believe the lies that our culture tells us about the trappings of success. Money and comfort and pleasure equal happiness. Comfort is such a high value in our society that no one wants to seem odd; no one wants to point out that people are giving their lives for what does not truly satisfy.

We need to listen to the voice of Jesus telling us that we still need him, even in our prosperity, and that there are riches that last far longer than anything we can work for here on earth.

☰ APPLY IT

Do you ever get too proud to receive help or constructive criticism?

Why is it easy, when life is fairly comfortable, to put your spiritual life on cruise control?

How can you keep spiritually vital even in a relatively wealthy and comfortable culture like ours?

46

AVOIDING THE PITFALLS
OF PROSPERITY

The online *Journal of the American Psychological Association* reported on a fascinating 2012 research project by Dr. Robert Kenny. He says, "Most of what we think we know about people with a lot of money comes from television, movies and beach novels – and a lot of it is inaccurate." [37]

In an effort to remedy that, Kenny, a developmental psychologist and senior advisor at the Center on Wealth and Philanthropy at Boston College, co-led a research project on the dilemmas of people worth $25 million or more. Kenny and his colleagues surveyed approximately 165 households via an anonymous online survey and were surprised to find that while money eased many aspects of these people's lives, it made other aspects more difficult.

Here is one of the questions they asked these wealthy people. "How does your money get in the way?" Dr. Kenny says, "We received response after response on how money is not always helpful." The takeaway from all of this, he says, is that you can't buy your way out of the human condition.

---

37 Amy Novotney, "Money Can't Buy Happiness", *Monitor on Psychology*, July/August 2012, Vol 43, No. 7; Print version: page 24, accessed at http://www.apa.org/monitor/2012/07-08/money.aspx

That's the bottom line. There are many benefits to wealth. When God blesses us with prosperity, and then we are generous to others, our money can have eternal impact. But it's not a cure for the human condition. As Augustine said, "Our hearts are restless until they find their rest in God."

That can even be difficult for Christians to remember. We can shift our attention from the beauty of the gospel to the problems and rewards of daily life. In his words to the Laodiceans, Christ advises a return to the riches of grace.

RETURNING TO THE RICHES OF GRACE

Jesus uses the language of a financial advisor when he says,

> *"So I advise you to buy gold from me — gold that has been purified by fire. Then you will be rich. Also buy white garments from me so you will not be shamed by your nakedness, and ointment for your eyes so you will be able to see."* REV. 3:18 NLT

Time for some more decoding. Again Jesus is using language the Laodiceans would have been familiar with, as he refers to their own banking and textile industries. He's saying, okay, I'll speak the language you love, the buzzwords of commerce. If you want goods of true quality, you need to do some business with me.

When he says, "Buy from me gold that has been purified by fire," he's referring to the fact that Laodicea was one of the first banking centers. People could literally "buy gold" from the Laodiceans. Travellers could bring bills of exchange here, scrolls that were much easier and safer to travel with than huge freight loads of precious metal or gems, and exchange them for gold at the Laodicean banks. Cicero writes that he did exactly this when he arrived in Laodicea in 51 BC.

Remarkably, the Laodiceans even minted their own money, with images not of Caesar but of themselves. Coins survive today from the time of Revelation with profiles of Laodicean citizens such as Julius Andronicus and several members of the Zenonid family. When you're *literally* making money, you know you're rich.

Some of the surrounding cities like Hierapolis and Colossae had also been minting their own coins (with images of Caesar and Greek gods, not of themselves) but production of their coins stopped abruptly at the time of the earthquake. Only Laodicean coins continued to gush out of their treasury even after that calamity.

GOOD GOLD

When Jesus urges them to do a money exchange for *his* kind of gold, a gold refined by fire, he is referring to the purest gold possible. It reminds me of what he says in Matthew 6:19-20:

> *"Don't store up treasures here on earth, where moths eat them and rust destroys them, and where thieves break in and steal. Store your treasures in heaven, where moths and rust cannot destroy, and thieves do not break in and steal."*

In other words, there is a kind of wealth that never loses its value — treasures you store in heaven. When you use your resources to help take care of the poor and needy and spiritually lost, you are exchanging volatile earthly currency for the best investment tool ever!

WHITE IS THE NEW BLACK

Then he counsels them to buy "white garments." The Laodiceans were so proud of their waterproof, black wool. They must have been pleased with how great they looked, and how their wool was the prized possession of so many.

The ancient historian Strabo wrote, "The country around Laodicea produces sheep remarkable not only for the softness of their wool...

but also for its raven-black color. And they get a splendid revenue from it..." [38]

But as wonderful as their wool was, it could never cover their sin. They had fallen from a focus on the riches of God's grace, becoming impressed instead with their own righteousness, interpreting their business success as evidence of God's approval. They were self-satisfied.

This is a subtle danger for all religious people.

As C.S. Lewis wrote,

> Prostitutes are in no danger of finding their lives so satisfactory that they find no need for God. It is the religious and self-righteous who are in that danger.

So Jesus reminds the Laodiceans that the clothing that really matters, in the long run, is the white garment we get from him by his grace. Throughout Revelation white clothes are associated with the people saved by Jesus' blood. As we've seen already, it's another call-out to previous apocalyptic books.

> *Though your sins are like scarlet,*
> *I will make them as white as snow.*
> *Though they are red like crimson,*
> *I will make them as white as wool.* ISAIAH 1:18 NLT

The Laodiceans were pretty impressed with themselves. And they were pretty sure God was impressed too. "Look at how God is blessing us. We are on a roll!"

But Jesus tells them the truth. They are being distracted. The riches that truly are worth prizing are the ones we receive from him! You can't buy your way out of the human condition.

---

38 Hemer, p. 199

≡ APPLY IT

How do the Christians at Laodicea see themselves? How does Jesus see them?

If Jesus told you the truth about your spiritual condition, what do you think he would say?

47

EYES TO SEE

E ye medicine was a big deal in Laodicea.

Ophthalmology was the fastest-growing branch of medicine in the Roman Empire when Revelation was written.

The area around Laodicea, the land of Phrygia, became famous for a concoction known as "Phrygian powder," an eye salve. The medical school here apparently specialized in this ointment.

Ancient coins from Laodicea honor Zeuxis, the founder of the medical school at Laodicea.

Demosthenes Philalethes was a famous graduate of this Laodicean medical school, and specialized in ophthalmology. His standard work on eye diseases was used as a medical text into medieval times.

Eye diseases were a subject of major experimentation in the first century. Two Roman doctors, Celsus and Scribonius Largus, wrote lengthy recipes for various eye salves in their works, which survive to this day. Their ingredients include metallic salts like copper, zinc, and alum. It's interesting that similar zinc compounds are used in modern eye treatments.

All the facts point to a widespread emerging practice of what we would call scientific medicine, cures for eye diseases based on experimentation and observation instead of magic. [39]

But the church in Laodicea, in a city which claimed to treat eye disease, was spiritually blind.

> *"I advise you to buy... ointment for your eyes so you will be able to see."* REV. 3:18B

God's diagnosis of their own inability to see their spiritual condition is this: Let me open your eyes so you can see both your need — and the riches I am offering.

EYE EXAM

Let's take the eye exam. Are we Laodiceans? Do we worship our commerce, our wealth, our comfort instead of Jesus?

Probably. In my case anyway. I love being comfortable. I like nice stuff. I am most definitely in danger of getting lukewarm. Every day of my life.

And this is dangerous, because passion is so important. No really great advance happens without a sense of need, of urgency, what athletes call "staying hungry". It is part of any great mission work or sacrificial giving or church plant or endurance through trial or great relationship or sports championship or career accomplishment. There has to be that spark of passion. When I get too comfortable, self-satisfied, lukewarm, I stop advancing.

So how do you reignite passion, or stay ignited? Jesus tells us next.

≡ APPLY IT

Ask Jesus to give you eyes to see your true spiritual condition, and the riches he offers by his grace to you every day.

---

39 Hemer, p. 197

48

OPEN THE DOOR

One of the most famous modern paintings of Jesus is William Hunt's "The Light of the World." It shows Jesus knocking on a wooden door. You've seen it. But have you noticed the details?

Weeds have grown up in front of the door. The hinges are rusted. Clearly that door has been closed for a while now. Fruit has been left to rot on the ground, instead of enjoyed.

Also, have you noticed there's no latch or doorknob on the outside of the door? It can only be opened from the inside.

And there's Jesus. Knocking. "Can anyone in there hear me anymore?"

That picture comes right out of his words to the Laodiceans. Despite their arrogance and self-sufficiency, Jesus still loves them. And his cure for their pride is so simple: Let's renew our friendship.

> "I correct and discipline everyone I love. So be diligent and turn from your indifference. Look! I stand at the door and knock. If you hear my voice and open the door, I will come in, and we will share a meal together as friends." REV. 3:19,20 NLT

This verse is especially striking when you know just a little more about Laodicea's history.

GUESTS THAT BARGE IN

Surviving ancient documents emphasize how frustrated the locals were that Roman governors and soldiers had the right to barge in and take over any house when they needed a place to stay while travelling. Since Laodicea was by far the wealthiest city with the nicest homes, Roman authorities repeatedly forced its wealthy residents to show them hospitality.

In one ancient record, a man named Polemo from Laodicea is outraged when he returns home from a business trip to discover that a Roman proconsul and his staff have taken over his mansion; in fact, Polemo is so upset he evicts them! This right to enforce hospitality was one of the most resented aspects of Roman rule in Laodicea.

JESUS IS A GENTLEMAN

In contrast, Jesus does not force anyone to show him hospitality. Though he is the ruler of the universe, he says, *"See? I stand at the door and knock."* He knows the antidote to our self-sufficiency is simple: A restored relationship with him. Spending time with him. Talking with him. Thanking him. Serving with him. But Jesus will not abuse his power as the Romans did. Jesus is a gentleman. You and I must open the door to him voluntarily. There is no coercion in Christianity.

When you renew your friendship with Jesus, when you begin to share life with him again as a conscious part of your daily walk, something happens quite naturally. Priorities begin to fall into place. Your perspective changes. How you want to spend your time changes. It all flows from a relationship with Jesus.

How do you start? Try reading the Bible daily. After this study ends, why not start reading a chapter of the gospels every day? Try Mark or John. Then pray. Start by just saying "Thanks" for a week. Let the relationship unfold.

When you begin to enjoy the riches of God's grace again, your passion is renewed. You enjoy rich times in prayer and in the word. You want to make an impact for Christ in the world. Not out of guilt but because of your friendship with Jesus.

For much of my young life I heard this verse quoted when non-believers were invited to make a commitment to Christ. But did you notice the context? This is written to Christians! They were believers who through a false sense of self-sufficiency had been keeping Christ out of their daily lives.

And this is Jesus' call to you. Can you hear him knocking? He does not say, "If you open the door I will sock you in the jaw or lecture you or make you feel guilty." He says, "Let's enjoy a meal together." He is your very best friend. Open the door to him again.

≡ APPLY IT

How can you open the door to Jesus right now?

How can you spend time with Jesus every day?

What gets in the way of doing this?

Although this was written to lukewarm believers, perhaps you are not sure if you've ever opened the door of your heart to Christ. Why not invite him in right now? You could pray something like this, if it reflects your heart's desire:

"Lord I need you. I am a sinner. Thank you that you love me so much you died and rose again to free me from sin. Help me understand this more and follow you more closely the rest of my life — and forever."

If you simply open the door, Christ promises to enter!

49

HEATED BACK UP

Did Christ's words have an impact on the church at Laodicea?

It appears so. Laodicea went on to become a major center of Christianity for centuries after the Book of Revelation was written. There are ancient records of 23 successive bishops of Laodicea. One of the Laodicean bishops helped formulate the Nicene Creed, the famous early summary of orthodox Christian beliefs composed in 325 AD. The last pastor of Laodicea whose name is recorded by history served in 1450 AD. At that point what little remained of the city was destroyed during the Turkish and Mongol invasions. But the church thrived for more than a thousand years.

That gives me hope. Christians who are lukewarm are not doomed to stay lukewarm. We can recover our passion and vision.

> *"Those who are victorious will sit with me on my throne, just as I was victorious and sat with my Father on his throne."* REV. 3:21

Victorious. It's the key word of the entire Book of Revelation. If you look for it, you'll see it again and again, not only at the end of each of these seven letters to seven churches, but in songs and promises through the rest of the book.

As we mentioned earlier in this book, the word is related to the Greek word *Nike*, from which we get the name for our modern shoe company. At the end of every grueling athletic competition in the ancient world, every marathon run or gladiator fight, there was a *nike* celebration where the victors would receive their reward.

Jesus is telling all these Christians in all seven churches, facing various challenges ranging from persecution to peer pressure to prosperity, to never give up, to keep their eyes on the goal, to think of the prize.

SEEING THE PROMISE

Now let your understanding of Jesus' message to the Seven illuminate the rest of Revelation. Many people find Revelation so impossible to understand that they never even try to read it. But try at least once to read it all the way through — without stopping to try and figure out what every little thing stands for. Look for overarching themes and repeated words and imagery.

What you are bound to discover is that the big picture of Revelation, the repeated theme, is that though believers will go through tribulation on earth, in Christ we are guaranteed the victory.

It is sometimes bad here on earth, sometimes very bad indeed, but it gets better, way better. Never give up! Christ will give you strength to win.

☰ APPLY IT

How is this an encouragement to you?

How can you encourage someone with this truth today?

50

KEEP LISTENING

"Anyone with ears to hear must listen to the Spirit and understand what he is saying to the churches." REV. 3:22

Have you listened? He still speaks today. How has the Living Jesus spoken to you through his message to *The Seven*? It's been said that every believer can go through stages similar to each of these churches. Where are you — and your church — right now?

EPHESUS: Busy as a bee, but I've left my first love. The cure? I can remember the passionate love for Jesus that once captured my heart, and do the things I did when I was first in love.

SMYRNA: I am poor and under pressure and persecution. I'm reminded that Jesus died and rose again, and is with me through it all. If I keep my eyes on him, I can remain faithful — and if I am not in Smyrna right now, I can pray for others undergoing persecution to stay faithful under pressure.

PERGAMUM: In a weird culture of diverse and strange beliefs, I resist cultural pressure to compromise, but I'm sloppy in my theology. I listen to false teachers, which will lead to a corruption of my character if I don't face up to this. I'm reminded that Jesus fights for the truth and promises me an eternal welcome.

THYATIRA: I am loving and faithful and serve others. I'm improving in so many ways. But in my enthusiasm I am not careful about the teaching I listen to, allowing false doctrine to creep in. That will lead to the death of my church unless I hold fast to the truth of the gospel.

SARDIS: I have a great reputation. But actually I'm nearly dead inside. If I don't wake up, trouble — and judgment — may sneak up on me like a thief. Jesus reminds me to wake up and stay alert. As he strengthens me, I can strengthen what remains alive.

PHILADELPHIA: I am weak. I am afraid. Earthquakes and persecution have shaken me to the core. But Jesus promises he will open doors for me. I can hold on tight to the gospel truth he has given me, endure these sufferings, and go on to great new opportunity.

LAODICEA: I have been blessed by a combination of good circumstances and my own pluck and hard work. I'm at the point where I feel self-sufficient. I don't feel I need anyone. But this is the core of my spiritual problem. I must realize my deep need for God, even in my comfort. He loves me and wants to be a regular guest in my heart again.

It's interesting to me that Jesus doesn't tell any of these churches to "do more." He says things like: *Come back to me, hang on, think deeper, wake up, open up.* All of his messages have to do with *internal* change, heart and mind and attitude shifts, not deeds. *Because the internal change leads to external change.* And God always works in that order.

The good news is, these churches seem to have responded well to Christ's messages. They all endured for many centuries with a vital role in the early faith. Just because things are not going well now does not mean your future is bleak. But like the first readers of *The Seven*, you and I need to listen to what Jesus says to the churches.

Ask God for continued ears to hear what he says to you through his Word.

≡ **APPLY IT**

What have you learned from our journey back into time and space as we've visited the ancient sites of the seven churches?

Which church or churches do you identify with now?

What has the Spirit said to you?

DISCUSSION QUESTIONS

You can watch free discussion starter videos filmed on location in Turkey at **www.tlc.org/theseven**

≡ DISCUSSION QUESTIONS

These questions are designed for a small group discussion following the videos, but feel free to use your own questions. The goal is to get your group thinking and sharing about the themes of these seven letters to the seven churches. Some questions call for deep introspection or analysis of the text. *Allow your group members time to ponder.* Silence in a group study is not "dead air". It is probably a sign that people are thinking through the implications of a verse or a point. Be patient.

WEEK 1

TO BUSY CHRISTIANS

☰ WARM UP

Introduce yourselves as you begin the first week of your seven-week journey of discovery.

What motivated you to be part of this study group? How do you hope to grow personally and what do you hope to learn?

How do you feel about studying part of the Book of Revelation?

What funny or intimidating ideas do people have about this book of the Bible?

One important note: While these are seven letters critiquing and encouraging seven actual churches, Christ's words here are not meant for you to use as ammunition to criticize other congregations. These are meant for us to apply to our own lives and our own church.

☰ READ & PRAY

Open your Bible to Revelation 2:1-7. Have someone in your group read the passage out loud. Pray that God will open your ears to hear what he says through these words.

Watch video #1 at www.tlc.org/theseven

☰ DISCUSS

1. What are the relational and spiritual dangers of a busy lifestyle?

2. Jesus has many words of praise for this church. What does he commend them for?

3. What fatal flaw does he see? Why is this so important to Jesus?

4. What can cause your first love for Jesus — that first enthusiastic passion you had when you understood the gospel — to leak away? Have you ever experienced this? What happened to drain that first love?

5. What do you think Jesus means by, "Remember the heights from which you have fallen"? How can this help any relationship? How can this help you spiritually?

6. What do you think Jesus means by, "do what you did at first"? How can this help any relationship? How can it help your relationship with Christ?

7. If your first love for Jesus was ever drained and then reignited, share with the group how you returned to a sense of love and passion for Christ. What helped? Does it parallel Christ's prescription for the Ephesians?

8. Is there a relationship right now that you need to reignite? How can you put Christ's words here into practice?

≡ WRAP UP

One goal for these studies is that each group will participate in some sort of group service project. Agree to pray about what that could be.

Ask for other prayer requests and write them down in the back of the book.

As you close, pray about issues that were raised during this discussion with your group.

WEEK 2

TO SUFFERING CHRISTIANS

≡ WARM UP

Share with one another how your week went. Also, share anything that struck you as interesting or surprising from the book so far.

≡ READ & PRAY

Open your Bible to Revelation 2:8-11. Pray that God will open your ears to hear what he says through these words.

Watch video #2 at www.tlc.org/theseven

≡ DISCUSS

1. Are you at a place in your life right now where you relate to Christ's words to this suffering church? Why?

2. Smyrna is one of the only churches in the Book of Revelation that has had an uninterrupted Christian presence for nearly 2,000 years since the book was written. This is intriguing, because in many ways, when Revelation was written, the future of this church seemed to be the most uncertain of them all. How does this encourage you?

3. What is it about Christ's description of himself here — that he is the First and the Last, that he died and came to life, that he knows our tribulation — that is encouraging to you?

4. Jesus does not say the Christians here will not suffer. In fact, he assures them that they will. But he says he will be with them, will

reward them, and that their suffering will have an end ("you will be tested... for ten days"). How is this a better encouragement than simply telling people that bright days are ahead?

5. Has your Christianity ever cost you anything — a job, an opportunity, a relationship, a business account? What happened? How did you see God bless despite this?

6. What are you afraid of right now? How do these words encourage you?

7. How would you summarize these words of Christ?

☰ WRAP UP

One goal for these studies is that each group will participate in some sort of group service project. Agree to pray about what that could be, and return next week to discuss it further.

Ask for prayer requests and write them down in the back of the book.

As you close, pray about issues that were raised during this discussion with your group.

WEEK 3

TO CONFUSED CHRISTIANS

≡ WARM UP

Share with one another how your week went.

What have you learned from a sermon, video, or devotional reading in this series? What has intrigued you or surprised you?

≡ READ & PRAY

Open your Bible to Revelation 2:12-17. Pray that God will open your ears to hear what he says through these words.

Watch video #3 at www.tlc.org/theseven

≡ DISCUSS

Jesus acknowledges the difficulty the Christians in Pergamum are facing. He knows they are living in a rather eclectic spiritual environment. It's dark. And they have been suffering. They have held on, even to the point of death. Yet even for them there is something Jesus wants to correct. Some of them have become followers of a cult-like teacher who insists they can compromise with their culture to the point of sexual immorality.

1. Why do you think such teaching would be attractive to people in a situation like theirs?

2. Are there times when suffering can actually weaken your resolve to resist temptation? Why? Have you ever seen this to be true in your own life?

3. The teachings of the Nicolaitans are obscure, but according to early Christian sources, they taught a form of "dualism" that states that what we do in the physical world does not impact our spiritual lives. Do you ever see people following a version of this today? How so?

4. It's important to note that Jesus does not criticize these Christians for living in Pergamum, or for doing business with pagans, or for knowing pagans as friends. In the video René said, "The problem was not that the church was in Pergamum, but that there was too much Pergamum in the church." How does this apply to us today? What practical steps can you take to try to be shaped more by Christ than by culture?

5. One of the lessons about Pergamum is that theology matters. How you think about God and the world — what you believe, the people you listen to — really does change your behavior. How have you seen your own beliefs about God impact your behavior?

6. What has been the core of your faith that has brought you back when you go astray, or kept you on the right track?

7. Are there lessons from Jesus' words to Pergamum that you feel are particularly relevant to your life?

☰ WRAP UP

Ask for prayer requests and write them down in the back of the book. As you close, pray about issues that were raised during this discussion with your group.

Before you leave, discuss your group service project. Share ideas. Your church may have plans for a service day, or a community impact day. Find out what opportunities may be there. If there seems to be consensus about an idea, make plans now for your group project.

WEEK 4

TO COMPROMISING CHRISTIANS

≡ **WARM UP**

Share with one another how your week went.

≡ **READ & PRAY**

Open your Bible to Revelation 2:18-29. Pray that God will open your ears to hear what he says through these words.

Watch video #4 at www.tlc.org/theseven

≡ **DISCUSS**

It's interesting that, of all the churches in *The Seven*, Thyatira is the one we know the least about. Fewer of its ruins survive. No Roman persecution is mentioned. The congregation was growing, full of love and faith and good works. Yet Jesus reserves his longest critique, by far, for this congregation.

1. Why is it important for Jesus to proclaim that he is the one "with feet like burnished bronze"? (see chapter 23)

2. This church is doing so many good works. But they have slowly drifted from the core of the gospel, and toward a false gospel taught by a self-proclaimed prophet that Jesus calls "Jezebel." He says that by her teaching she misleads people into immorality. In these seven letters you consistently see the importance Jesus places on teaching, and not just behavior. Why is doctrine so important

to God? Why does it matter what I believe as long as I am doing good works? (Hint: Think long-term)

3. Jesus says the cultic leaders at Thyatira are teaching the "so-called deep secrets of Satan." Why is "secret" teaching so appealing to people? How do you see this today?

4. The Thyatirans were ultimately facing pressure to conform, not from Roman government persecution, but from the business world. Are there similar temptations to compromise associated with career and the workplace in our society?

5. Have you ever been tempted to compromise at work in some way? If you feel comfortable, share with the group what happened. How did you resist, or give in and then come back?

6. Obviously God understands that many Christians will be working with and for people who may not share their values. How can you maintain Christian integrity in the workplace without unnecessarily driving everyone around you crazy? Look up 1 Peter 3:15,16 and have someone read it to the group. What advice do these verses give about how to preserve your Christian witness when surrounded by people who do not share your faith?

7. Jesus has some harsh-sounding words for the Thyatirans, but we need to remember that, first, he says he has given this false teacher time to repent. He is always patient with us. If there are no consequences to our sin immediately apparent, that does not mean God approves. It means God is patient. Second, he sometimes lets us hit bottom in order for us to give up and turn our lives over to him. Have you ever been glad to hit bottom because it brought you to God – or have you seen this happen to a friend or loved one? If you are comfortable, and can do so without breaking confidences, share what happened.

8. What is your biggest take-away from this letter to Thyatira?

≡ WRAP UP

Ask for prayer requests and write them down in the back of the book. As you close, pray about issues that were raised during this discussion with your group.

Before you leave, discuss your group service project. If you've already had a chance to serve, discuss your feelings about the project. What was challenging about it? What was fun?

WEEK 5

TO DEAD CHRISTIANS

≡ WARM UP

Share with one another how your week went.

What was your favorite part of the reading since last week? Did anything intrigue you or surprise you?

≡ READ & PRAY

Open your Bible to Revelation 3:1-6. Pray that God will open your ears to hear what he says through these words.

Watch video #5 at www.tlc.org/theseven

≡ DISCUSS

1. Has your faith ever been dead and yet come back to life? Why? What happened to kill it and then how was it brought back?

2. Is there now a gap between your reputation and your reality in some area of your life? Where?

3. It's interesting that Jesus doesn't mention any external or internal problems that the Sardis Christians were facing, unlike most of the other churches in *The Seven*. There's no mention of persecution or false doctrine or compromise or other suffering. How is a comfortable life sometimes a challenge to spiritual growth? Could this be a challenge in our culture now?

4. How does Jesus advise the Sardis Christians to change? What do you think "strengthen what remains" means practically? How could this work in a relationship with a spouse or child?

5. Jesus tells them to "Remember, therefore, what you have received and heard; hold it fast..." He is telling them to remember the gospel they heard and received. Why is it important for us Christians to keep preaching the gospel to ourselves? How does this help our faith stay alive? Have you ever found your faith revitalized by a simple return to the gospel of grace?

6. How do Jesus' words encourage you, particularly if you find yourself in a place where your faith is on life support?

≡ WRAP UP

If you haven't had a chance to discuss it yet, talk about your group service project. If you've completed it since your last meeting, how did it go? What did you find challenging? What was fun?

Pray about issues that were raised during this discussion with your group. Ask for prayer requests and write them down in the back of the book.

WEEK 6

TO DISCOURAGED CHRISTIANS

☰ WARM UP

Share with one another how your week went.

What did you read this week in the book that interested you or challenged you?

☰ READ & PRAY

Open your Bible to Revelation 3:7-13. Pray that God will open your ears to hear what he says through these words.

Watch video #6 at www.tlc.org/theseven

☰ DISCUSS

1. Do you remember experiencing an actual earthquake or other natural disaster, as the Philadelphian Christians did? How did it impact your sense of security?

2. Have you ever been discouraged when one thing after another seems to go wrong in life? What helped you?

3. Jesus tells these discouraged people, hammered by earthquakes, bad government, persecution, and more, some very encouraging things:

- First, he tells them that he is the "true" one, meaning he will stay true and faithful. He will not betray them. How would this encourage you if you were in their situation?

- Next he tells them he "knows your works." How is it encouraging to a suffering, persecuted minority to hear that God knows what good they are doing?

- He promises them that they will be "pillars." How was this an image of comfort particularly to these people?

- Then he says he will write on them three things: The name of God, the name of the city of God, and Jesus' own heavenly name. It's a poetic way of reminding them what to "tattoo" on their hearts. The worship of the true God, the hope of the eternal city, and the love of Jesus for us is where we find our strength. How is this a comfort to suffering people?

4. If you have undergone times of suffering, what particularly was it about your faith that was important for your endurance? Does it relate to any of the things Jesus tells the Philadelphians here?

5. What can Christ's words tell us about how to pray for and comfort those going through times of trouble?

6. How does it encourage you to know that this tiny band of suffering Christians became a consistent witness of Christ, sending missionaries to the world for centuries after this was written?

≡ WRAP UP

Take time now to pray for Christians suffering persecution around the globe, particularly those in the Middle East.

If you haven't had a chance to discuss it yet, talk about your group service project. If you've completed it since your last meeting, how did it go? What did you find challenging? What was fun?

Pray about issues that were raised during this discussion with your group. Ask for prayer requests and write them down in the back of the book.

WEEK 7

TO INDIFFERENT CHRISTIANS

≡ WARM UP

Share with one another how your week went.

What have you learned so far in this study that has made the biggest impression on you? Have you seen changes or growth?

≡ READ & PRAY

Open your Bible to Revelation 3:14-22. Pray that God will open your ears to hear what he says through these words.

Watch video #7 at www.tlc.org/theseven

≡ DISCUSS

1. The Laodiceans had it good. They were the richest and most comfortable of all the churches in *The Seven*. Yet what does Jesus say about them in these verses?

2. These seven letters say a lot to Christians facing suffering. But affluent Christians face their own challenges. How can comfort and a sense of self-reliance threaten a vital faith?

3. How are you doing in this area? Have you ever felt as if a focus on self-reliance and your own achievement has kept you from realizing your need for God? Does a love of comfort ever interfere with your commitment to serve God?

4. If you have been revitalized from a period of being "lukewarm," what happened? How was your heart turned toward him?

5. Jesus tells the Laodiceans to realize life's true treasures. What are the "hidden treasures" that affluent people can sometimes undervalue?

6. Jesus also tells them to receive his correction. It's easy in our pride to think every word of correction in the Bible applies to someone else, and not us. Why is this so? How can we overcome this tendency?

7. Jesus ends with an almost heartbreaking picture of himself, the Lord of the Universe, patiently standing at the door of our hearts, knocking, waiting for us to open up. What does this tell you about Jesus?

8. It's interesting that this invitation to open the door to Jesus is written not to unbelievers, but to Christians. How is it possible to be saved, to be a believer, and yet not have fellowship daily with Jesus? Have you ever been there? What helped you?

9. What main images or ideas from this study have impacted your life? What do you hope to take with you on your life's journey?

≡ WRAP UP

Pray about issues that were raised during this discussion with your group. Ask for prayer requests and write them down in the back of the book.

RESOURCES

Tom Holladay, Brad Johnson, Doug Fields, and Todd Wendorff, *The 7 Churches of Revelation*, sermon series preached at Saddleback Church, Orange County, 2000

Exploring Ephesus (DVD by Christian History Institute distributed by Vision Video)

Colin J. Hemer, *The Seven Letters to the Seven Churches of Asia in Their Local Setting* (Grand Rapids: Eerdman's, 1989)

Robert Murray M'Cheyne, *The Seven Churches of Asia* (Geanies House, Great Britain: Christian Focus, reprinted 2008)

William Ramsay, *The Seven Letters to the Seven Churches* (Grand Rapids: Baker Book House, reprinted 1985)

Mark Wilson, *Victory Through The Lamb: A Guide to Revelation in Plain Language* (Wooster, Ohio: Weaver Book Co., 2014)

In addition to these books, I was very influenced by sermons from John MacArthur, Rick Warren, Ray Stedman, Ray Pritchard, Charlie Dyer, Ray Johnston, Curt Harlow, John Ortberg, Mark Driscoll, and many, many others. Driscoll's series on Rev. 2 and 3 was particularly helpful for our video scripts. I don't agree with everything all of these men say (I don't agree with everything I hear myself saying sometimes!) but I have a memory for the well-turned phrase and feel certain that there were huge swaths of material in this book where I essentially regurgitated what I heard and memorized from some or all of these pastors.

THANKS

Special thanks to my awesome family, especially my wife Laurie and son David, who joined me on our church trip to the sites of these seven churches and helped in innumerable ways on the journey. I grew to know and love everyone who joined us on that amazing three week journey!

Thanks also to the wonderful staff at Twin Lakes Church, particularly Valerie Webb, who helped keep me on track throughout this project and provided excellent feedback; Jamie Rom, who videotaped and photographed the sites when we visited in October 2014; Kevin Deutsch, whose graphic expertise created a beautiful book layout, and Adrian Moreno for his great work on the book cover. My fellow pastor at Twin Lakes, Mark Spurlock, preached excellent sermons on Pergamum and Laodicea that I found very helpful. Karen O'Connor and Adam Nigh proofread an early draft and provided many enormously valuable suggestions. Martin Olander expertly produced the audio tracks for the videos and audio book.

And of course we could not have done this without the wonderful people at Levent Oral's Tutku Tours in Turkey. For the majority of our time there Tulu Gökkadar served as the best guide I could ever have imagined for this project.